Holiday Cycling around Anglesey and Caernarfon

LYN GOODKIN

Hobbyhorse
B○○KS

By the same author

Family Cycling in North Cheshire and Around its Borders
Family Cycling in West Cheshire and Wirral

First Published in 1995 by Hobbyhorse Books
The Old Post Office, Chester Road, Daresbury, Warrington, Cheshire, WA4 4AJ

Although every effort has been made to ensure that the details are correct at the time of going to press the author and publisher cannot accept any responsibility for any inaccuracies or omissions. While potentially dangerous junctions have been indicated by '**with care**' in the text, all cycling is potentially dangerous with the increased traffic at the present time. The author and publisher cannot be held responsible for accidents to anyone following the routes described in this volume. It is especially important for parents and guardians to be responsible for the safety of their children when cycling.

Opening times and entrance charges change as do landmarks and even the names of pubs. The author would be grateful to hear from any cyclist who spots any changes or with helpful suggestions for future updates of this work.

Cover photographs by Alan Goodkin
All other photographs by the author
Illustrations on pages 20, 61, 78, 104, 125 and 132 by Janet Goodkin
Illustrations on pages 8, 10, 11 and 18 by James Fisher

Printed by Manchester Free Press, Thomas Street, Stretford, Manchester, M32 0JT

FOREWORD

Growing up in Anglesey, with a very keen cyclist for a father, my brother and I were introduced early on to the pleasures and opportunities for exploration by bicycle. As we wobbled along on our first bikes, later progressing to larger models and—when our legs grew long enough—helping to power the family's ancient tandem, we gradually came to know many of the island's roads and lanes and had our own favourites, as did so many of our friends. Sheltered lanes with tall hedges and trees for hot or windy days, open rides along the rocky bones of the island for clear days in spring and autumn when the views out to sea and over to the mainland are so stunning, quiet tracks down to the sea for summer and winter alike. Our bikes were the unquestioned form of transport, for private or group expeditions, for visiting friends and relatives, and for day-dreaming journeys into the imagination. And now, working on the coast of Anglesey, I am pleased to see the increasing popularity of cycling.

Nowadays the roads are generally much busier, some out of all recognition, with traffic thundering along the main ones, and more effort must be made to find safe lanes and quiet routes suitable for cycling, especially for those unfamiliar with the area or who are not regular cyclists. And here is the ideal book to help—with clear and entertaining descriptions of twenty rides on Anglesey and the mainland. Browsing through the book will inspire many families to take the plunge and explore new areas, and the inclusion of routes of different lengths—and short cuts, for when unused muscles complain or children suddenly tire!—will enable cyclists of greatly differing ability and experience to enjoy this means of getting around. The more energetic may wish to link routes together to make interesting longer outings.

This book should appeal to local cyclists and visitors from further afield, and I have great pleasure in commending it to everyone who will appreciate the effort that Lyn Goodkin has put into researching the routes and presenting them in such an agreeable and informative way.

Rhiannon Jones

ACKNOWLEDGEMENTS

Many thanks to the following for all their help:

SUSTRANS and John Grimshaw for information on the National Cycleway proposals.

Gwynedd County Council for information on cycleway proposals for the county and especially Rhys Roberts, John Lazarus and the Highways Department for information, for taking cyclists' interests seriously and for help in checking the definitive maps of the area.

Don and Barbara Roscoe for trying out some of the instructions.

Les Goulding, Rhiannon Jones and Rob Brown for help with the Glossary of Welsh terms.

Rhiannon Jones of Anglesey Coastal Heritage for advice.

Ruth Goodkin for reading the text and suggesting improvements.

And last but not least Alan Goodkin for much help, sometimes putting a spoke in, but never a spanner in the works!

CONTENTS

THE RIDES

ANTICLOCKWISE AROUND THE ISLE OF ANGLESEY

COASTAL ARFON

KEY TO MAP SYMBOLS

▬▬▬	Motorway or dual carriageway	✳	place of interest
▬▬▬	A road	PH	public house
▬▬▬	other road or lane	P	car park
▬ ▬ ▬ ▬ ▬	Bridleway, Road Used as a Public Path, By-way Open to All Traffic, cycle lane, or rough track.	⌒⌒	river or coast
		⬭	lake
· · · · · · · · · · ·	footpath	+	church or chapel
▬●▬	railway line and station	→	direction of main route

INTRODUCTION

With the help of this guide you should be able to find plenty of wonderful cycling routes to suit most abilities. Since mountain bikes have become so popular many people are looking for good **off-road rides**. I hope this book will help you find the best of these in the area.

The lanes on Anglesey are very quiet and often amazingly free of traffic outside the main holiday season. We have 'discovered' a few tracks on which you will enjoy riding mountain bikes. In the coastal part of Arfon there are several **bridleways** and **roads used as public paths (RUPPs)**, on which cycling is legally permitted, and three excellent **cycleways**, which are designed for shared use with pedestrians and in some cases horse riders.

Actually Anglesey has very few bridleways or RUPPs, the only ones being found in the parish of Llanddona, and even these are not marked on the OS map. I have included a sketch of their location but they are disappointing. Since there are no canals there are obviously no towpaths. This guide should help the off-road cycle enthusiast or parents wanting safe traffic free cycling for themselves and their children to find what is available at present.

I lived in the area for 4 years and have holidayed in Anglesey every year since then, based in Menai Bridge. We have ridden all these routes at least twice and sometimes rather more than twice! We have been out at all seasons and in varied weather so the routes have been well checked from a cyclist's point of view, both literally and metaphorically.

My first two cycle touring guides were, *Family Cycling in North Cheshire and Nearby Areas* and *Family Cycling in West Cheshire and Wirral*. Cycling in North Wales makes an interesting contrast to cycling in Cheshire. The terrain even on Anglesey and certainly in Arfon is more undulating: Cheshire is really very flat! The routes are carefully planned to avoid hills as far as possible, but some are unavoidable. The direction of the routes is to give shorter sharper ascents and thus longer gentle descents.

During the last few years many more families have started taking bicycles on holiday with them to North Wales. The popularity of caravans and camper vans for the family holiday all make cycling an easy holiday activity. The ease of taking bikes on roof or boot racks or on tow bar attachments makes it possible for the whole family's bikes to go on holiday too. It is mainly for the visitors to Anglesey, who may not be familiar with all the inland rural lanes suitable for cycling, that this guide is written. I hope that many residents will also find it useful and discover some different routes and plan variations to their cycle rides.

The lengths of the routes are purposely kept fairly short so they are suitable for all comers but many of them can be linked together to provide more challenging runs for the fitter or more experienced cyclist—a **round the**

Cycling incentives

island trip can be planned using the overall map, Rides 3-8, 10-15 and the relevant links. If you are new to cycling or returning to it after many years, or are taking children then don't be put off by distances of eg 15 miles. It is much easier on a bike of course than walking and even at slow speeds of 5-7 miles an hour you can cover this distance in 2-3 hours—a pleasant half day outing. Some routes are shorter than this and some have short cuts. Some, such as on the cycleway from Caernarfon, can be done as there-and-back rides so you can go just as far as the muscles or the children want! As your fitness improves or for older children you will want to increase your distances; these routes are designed to allow this by having extra loops or by linking two or more routes together. Cycle club outings regularly cover 50 miles or more in a day!

I cycle mainly with my husband and with whichever friends and family can join us. It is obviously easier cycling in small groups of matched age or ability. If you have a large group some will have to cycle slower and some faster than they would as individuals or you will need to have rendezvous points. This guide should help. You will need to ensure children in your care have good road sense and the necessary cycling skills!

DESIGN OF ROUTES

The Rides fall loosely into three areas:

Northern and Central Anglesey   Rides 1-9 and 15
Southern Anglesey   Rides 10-14
Coastal Arfon   Rides 16-20

Several rides interlink, mainly in the groupings above to avoid crossing the A5 so really challenging distances can be attempted by the superfit! Some of the routes can link up with the projected NCR for people wanting even longer rides.

Many routes pass caravan parks and many should be accessible directly from home as they are quite near to centres of population, as follows:

Menai Bridge: 1, 2, 14, 15, and 17
Bangor: 15, 16 and 17
Bethesda: 16
Caernarfon: 18, 19 and 20
Benllech area: 3 and 4
Llangefni: 3 and 15
Amlwch and the north: 5, 6, 7, 8 and 9
Holyhead: 10
Rhosneigr, Aberffraw and the south west: 11, 12 and 13.

A few of the rides are near or pass a railway station and most also have a public car park at the recommended start for anyone bringing bikes by car.

Several **alternatives** make for complicated sounding instructions, but they aren't too difficult, since on each occasion you will only be following your one chosen alternative. I think that it is essential for cycle touring routes to have shorter and longer possibilities as peoples', especially children's, abilities vary. This also provides emergency short cuts and variety for different days' outings and allows for progress in distance travelled. Everyone enjoys the challenge of trying to go a few miles further next time!

Distances are given in kilometres as well as miles. Distances are provided for the whole route, short cuts and separate loops.

Ascents are given in metres. Total ascents added together sound worse than they really are since they are spread out in separate hills with flat places and descents in between!

Individuals' **speed** will vary. It is useful to time your own group to help planning, for example to make sure you get back in the light, to plan the time of arrival at places with definite closing times (the tourist attractions

Check opening times

and shops as well as the pubs!). Many of the **tourist attractions** on Anglesey are closed on Mondays (except Bank Holidays), although Plas Newydd closes on Saturdays instead. Without stops you can expect to do about 8-10 miles an hour. Fast cyclists can easily do 12 miles or more an hour. If you want to visit a certain place at a certain time then you might be able to change the starting point to somewhere a suitable distance from your objective as most of these are circular tours.

Suitable **off-road routes** are hard to find on Anglesey but whatever is available at the present has been included. Short sections of **bridleway and cycleway** are included, mostly with a road alternative for those with light bikes or for those who prefer to stay on a good surface. Although there are other bridleways (especially in the Port Dinorwic area) I haven't included them as they are across muddy fields which can be difficult sometimes, depending on whether they have been ploughed, have pasture or have crops growing. Some may, however, be suitable at certain times. Stiles can be a problem, to cyclists as well as horses! For a few routes, the off-road sections are an integral, major or unavoidable part of the route: such as ¾ mile on Ride 8, 1 mile on Ride 11, ½ mile on Ride 12, 6 miles on Ride 13, 3 miles on Ride 16, 4 miles on Ride 18, 6 miles on Ride 19, and 11 miles on Ride 20.

Unavoidable crossings of main roads and a few roundabouts are marked **'with care'** in the text. If there are too many of these in a particular Ride then don't do this route with younger or less experienced children. It may be necessary to accompany children individually across such roads as common sense dictates at the time. There is a need for cycle lanes around roundabouts and along some trunk roads, especially the A5. As well as recommending and enthusing about certain routes in this area I have also pointed out any problems that we have found—there aren't many! Although this may seem negative I feel it is just as important in this sort of guide.

Bike hire is available at White Gables in Rhosneigr (only a few bikes). There may be others which we have not discovered.

Further afield, you can hire bikes at Beddgelert Forest, Hafod Ruffydd Uchaf, tel 01766 86454. Follow signs from the Forestry Commission Campsite on the Beddgelert to Caernarfon Road. In July and August they are also in the campsite from 9-10, 1-2 and 4.30-5. Bikes can also be hired at Beics Betws, Tan Lan, Betws y Coed, and even further away at Lake Bala.

Check the route

Although route maps are given for each ride I would recommend you to refer to the relevant Landranger series **Ordnance Survey maps** (scale 2cm to 1km) as these will also provide the route from your home base, other alternatives and other information, eg the extent of built up areas and contours. The two to accompany this book are **Sheet 114 Anglesey for Rides 1-15, 17 and part of 16, and Sheet 115 Snowdon and Surrounding Area for Rides 1-3 and 14-20**. Some of the suggestions for other rides use Sheet 116 Denbigh and Colwyn Bay.

With **children** it is best to start with short rides and, depending on how they enjoy it, to increase the length of routes gradually. The same might well be said by some children of their parents! At a young age children prefer to stop frequently for a rest and for a mental as well as a physical diversion. Because of their small size children lose heat more rapidly than adults so be prepared for extra care in cold and windy weather. A recent survey has shown that children are not doing enough physical exercise and many are becoming 'couch potatoes'! Cycling can be an excellent way for children to do an enjoyable form of exercise at whatever level of exertion is appropriate for them.

Taking Your Bike by Train. In previous guides I have given at least one railway station for each ride so that cyclists could use the train to reach a route if it was too far from home and avoid if possible using a car on quiet country lanes.

However the provision for cyclists has now deteriorated even further as to be mostly prohibitive at £3 per journey with compulsory reservation. Not all trains accept bikes. Except for a few services the Crewe-Holyhead line will only carry 1 bike per train. A few trains have space for up to 10 bikes. The leaflet *Cycling by Train* lists these. Also in Anglesey and coastal Arfon there aren't very many stations. I have marked the location of convenient stations on the route maps. Cyclists able to do longer distances will be able to reach other Rides besides these listed as having a station en route:

Bangor for Rides 16 and 17, Llanfairpwll for Rides 1, 2 and 15, Rhosneigr and Bodorgan for Ride 11, Ty Croes for Ride 12, and Holyhead for Ride 10.

CYCLEWAYS FOR NORTH WALES

NATIONAL CYCLE ROUTE (NCR)

SUSTRANS and Groundwork have exciting plans for a proposed NCR through this part of North Wales. It is provisionally supported by Gwynedd County Council but obviously details and finances have to be finalised. It will start at Holyhead. There are problems to overcome in avoiding the A5. There are plans to provide a cycle route through **Penrhos Coastal Park** on Holy Island to link Holyhead to Valley and for cyclists to be able to use the footway over the Stanley embankment. Then between Valley and Llanfihangel yn Nhowyn some provision is needed to avoid the A5. After that the proposed route follows some of the pleasant quiet lanes we use in this guide through the villages of Engedi, Dothan, Soar and Bethel to cross the Afon Cefni like we do by Pont Marquis. It continues via Llangaffo, Llanddaniel Fab and Llanfairpwll. To cross the Menai Strait it is hoped to negotiate with Railtrack use of the Britannia Bridge service road. This is the most interesting suggestion as it would give cyclists a much safer bridge segregated from traffic.

Once on the mainland one proposal is to negotiate a route round the Vaynol estate to reach Port Dinorwic. Most of the railway path, **Lôn Las**, from here to Caernarfon has recently been or is about to be completed. From Caernarfon it follows, as we do, the **Lôn Eifion** cyclepath south down the Lleyn Peninsula. At present there are a large number of access controls (I have mentioned the gates etc in my notes for Rides 19 and 20) which would slow down a long distance tourer but aren't too much of a problem for short distance holiday cyclist. Also the surface and width deteriorate quite a lot just south of Llanllyfni so the suggestion is to take the lanes just to the east of the A487 through the villages of Nebo, Nazareth, Pant Glâs, Dolbenmaen and Golan (there are some 'Heights' here too but mostly the lanes contour round them!). And so south to Criccieth. The main problem of this idea is that there are several main road crossings. New tracks may be constructed between Criccieth and Porthmadog. At present using the beach near Borth-y-Gest is the best option. The route from here to mid and south wales is out of the territory of this guide. For further information send a donation to SUSTRANS! If it has the go-ahead it will form part of a 5000 mile network of cycle routes in Britain. SUSTRANS has applied to the Millennium Fund for help with this much needed scheme.

LONYDD GLAS YN ARFON/LÔN LAS ARFON

The **Port Dinorwic/Y Felinheli to Caernarfon** cyclepath is almost finished. The Caernarfon to Plas Menai (Griffith's Crossing new roundabout) section

Lôn Eifion

opened Easter 1995 and the next section will soon, depending on finance. Other short sections are already open (see Ride 17).

The **Bangor to Glasinfryn** cyclepath is lovely and ideal for family outings. It is short in terms of a through route and leads to main roads at the moment. It is not adequately signed at present and is unfortunately incorrectly placed on the OS map on the wrong disused railway! It has recently been extended to Port Penrhyn and it is hoped that the extension to Bethesda will open in 1996. It was created in the late 1980s by 'Gwynedd Cycle Routes' with the help of a Manpower Services Commission Project. It is now being extended and maintained by Arfon Borough Council.

Lôn Eifion

The name is derived from the area traditionally known as Eifionydd in which the southern section of the route is located. The track runs from Caernarfon to Bryncir at present and we use it on Rides 18, 19 and 20. Unfortunately the section south of Bryncir is in private ownership. The path was studied by the Countryside Management section of Gwynedd County Council's Economic Development and Planning Department in May 1993 for its wildlife value. It was found to be a haven for all sorts of wildlife. A total of 173 different plants were found including herbs, shrubs, trees, mosses and lichens. It was one of 27 sites of special interest looked at in detail with the aim of providing the council with an environmental management plan. The plan suggests when trees, coppices, and undergrowth should be cut back for the benefit of the wildlife as a whole. Cyclists benefit from a good management plan as not only does it keep the dreaded thorny hawthorns in check but enhances the environment and provides a refuge for interesting wildlife to see when quietly cycling along. For further information tel 01286 830222.

If the proposal to reopen the Welsh Highland Railway is passed then the Caernarfon to Dinas section (just south of Bontnewydd) would be constructed on Lôn Eifion and the cyclepath would be relaid parallel to it. This would change the nature of the path and its scenery and during construction it is likely that parts of the cyclepath might be closed for certain times. However a potential benefit might be that cycles could be carried on the trains so that cyclists could do linear routes and return by train.

Also a possible future cycleway could follow the general route of this **Welsh Highland Railway** from Caernarfon via Dinas, Beddgelert and the Aberglaslyn Pass to Porthmadog, using minor roads, forest tracks and a path running beside the railway which may be re-opened. All this, even if it happens, is a few years into the future. Dream on!

For further information contact Mr R Roberts (Gwynedd County Council, tel 01286 679305).

PUNCTURES

Most punctures on Anglesey lanes seem to be due to the thorns from hawthorn hedges. Our experience is that this is mainly a problem in autumn and sometimes also in spring after hedgecutting. It is well worth avoiding riding over hedge cuttings lying at the side of the lanes provided this can be done safely without riding too far out into the centre of the road. Mountain bike or 'hybrid' tyres are much thicker and resist all but the longest thorns. Anti-puncture tape can help but we found it eventually causes chafing at the edges followed by punctures! There may be better tape available now.

EASY AND INFALLIBLE GUIDE TO PUNCTURE REPAIR

1   Remove the wheel, making a note of which side of the frame the washers go. If a rear wheel on a derailleur bike, change to a high gear, pull the changer back against its spring, remember where the axle goes in relation to the chain and lift wheel out. If a Sturmey-Archer unscrew the gear cable.
2   Take dust cap and nut off valve.
3   Lever off the tyre from the rim.
4   Remove the inner tube, noting which way round it is.
5   Inflate inner tube until you can hear or feel air coming out of the puncture (if necessary, immerse in water or spit on it and look for bubbles).
6   Mark the hole with pen or wax crayon; make bigger marks than the area of glue. Or stick a pin in the hole—don't worry, it's a hole anyway!
7   Deflate the remaining air from the tyre.
8   Dry the area and rub down with sand paper.
9   Apply rubber solution to an area slightly bigger than the patch.
10 Leave it to become dry and tacky—don't be impatient.
11 Peel backing paper off the patch (some also have foil which needs removing with a pen knife after the patch has stuck).
12 Stick patch on firmly and don't try to lift its edges up again. Grate a little chalk over the patch to stop the glue sticking to the tyre. It is easier to use sandpaper for this than the inadequate grater on the tin!
13 Feel and look around the inside of the tyre to find the cause of the puncture. Remove any thorns etc.
14 Check for a second puncture but do not over inflate the inner tube while it is not protected by the tyre.

15 Partially inflate the inner tube.

16 Put the valve in its hole first and put the inner tube back into the rim. Make sure that the rim tape is still in place.

17 Starting near the valve push the tyre back into the rim making sure that the inner tube is not trapped. You should be able to do this using your thumbs only and not the tyre levers. Check that the tyre is evenly seated all the way round on both sides.

18 Inflate a little more, but not too much, or you won't be able to get it past the brake blocks.

19 Reseat the wheel in the forks or drop-out.

20 Tighten the wheel nuts thumb tight, spin the wheel to make sure that it does (ie that it isn't skewed)!

21 Tighten with a spanner.

22 Fully inflate the tyre.

Even better, replace the punctured inner tube with the spare one you have brought and mend the puncture in comfort and at leisure at home! But don't forget to remove the cause of the puncture first.

WHAT TO TAKE

this book!	puncture repair kit	tools
tyre levers	pump	spare inner tube
old rag/old glove/bit of bent wire for dealing with oily chain		
allen keys	waterproofs	spare warm clothing
OS map	drink	first aid kit
helmet	money	food

light high energy foods such as fruit cake, dried fruit, bananas and chocolate (omit the chocs in hot weather!)

A gadget called Kwikstik could be a useful addition to tyre levers.

In winter, wear warmer clothes on your icycle!

GLOSSARY OF WELSH FOR CYCLISTS

aber - river, mouth
ac eithrio - except for access
afon - river
agored - open
allanfa argyfwng - emergency exit
allt - hill, wood
anifeiliaid - animals
araf - slow
bach - small
bae - bay
beic/beiciau - bicycle/s
beiciwr/beicwyr - cyclist/s
beicwyr man disgyn - cyclists'
     dismounting place
bore da - good morning
bryn - hill, rise
bwlch - pass, gap
bychan/fechan - small
cae - field
caer - fort
capel - chapel
carreg - stone
castell - castle
cefn - ridge, at the back of
cerrig - stones
cilfan argyfwng - emergency layby
coch - red
coed - wood
cors - marsh
craig - rock
crib - ridge
croeslon - crossroads
croes - cross
croeso - welcome
dim beicio - no cycling
dim gwersyllu dros nôs - no
     overnight camping
dinas - fort
diolch yn fawr - thank you

diwedd - end
du/ddu - black
dŵr - water
dyffryn - valley
dynion - gents
eglwys - church
ffordd - road, way
ffordd ddeuol - dual carriageway
ffynnon - well, spring
glan - shore
glas - blue (green field)
glyn - valley
gwasanaethau - services
gwen/gwyn/wen/wyn - white
gwynt - wind
gwylfa/wylfa - look-out
gwyrdd - green
hên - old
hir - long
ildiwch - give way
isaf - lower
llan - church, parish
llath - yards
llwybr cyhoeddus - public footpath
llwyd - grey
llyn - lake
lôn ar agor - lane open
lôn ar gau - lane closed
maes - open field
mawr - big
melin - mill
merched - ladies
milltir - miles
môr - sea
moel - rounded hill
mynydd - mountain
nant - valley, brook
newydd - new
nos da - good night

o'ch blaen - ahead
pant - valley, hollow
parc - field, parkland
pen - head, top
penrhyn - headland
pentre - village
perygl - danger
plas - mansion
pont/bont - bridge
porth - harbour, gateway
pwll - pond
rhos - moorland

rhyd - ford
sarn - causeway
talwch yma - pay here
traeth - beach
tref - town
tŷ/ty - house
uchaf - upper
wedi cau - closed
y/yr - the
ynys - island
Ynys Môn - Anglesey
ysbyty - hospital

ddraid - dragon

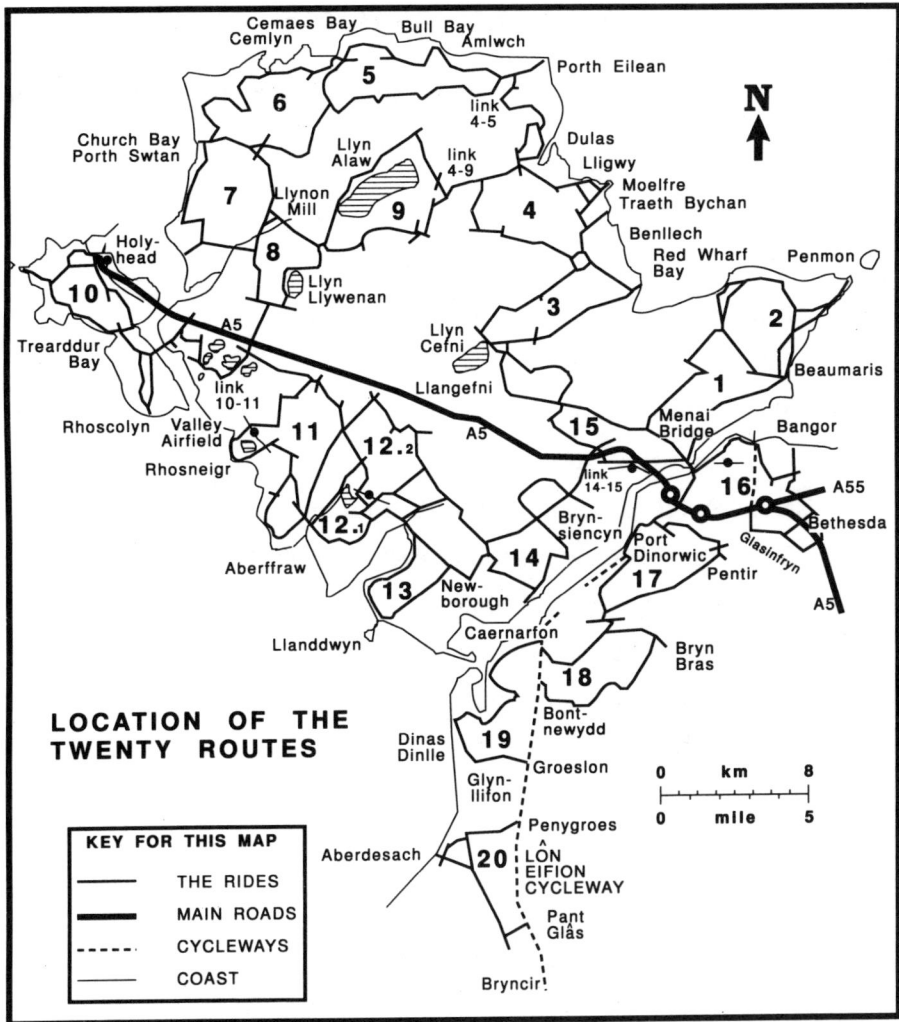

LOCATION OF THE
TWENTY ROUTES

KEY FOR THIS MAP

——	THE RIDES
▬▬	MAIN ROADS
----	CYCLEWAYS
——	COAST

Cemaes Bay
Cemlyn
Bull Bay
Amlwch
Porth Eilean
5
6
link 4-5
Church Bay
Porth Swtan
Llyn Alaw
link 4-9
Dulas
Lligwy
7
Llynon Mill
9
4
Moelfre
Traeth Bychan
8
Benllech
Holy-head
Llyn Llywenan
Red Wharf Bay
Penmon
10
3
2
A5
Llyn Cefni
1
Beaumaris
Trearddur Bay
Llangefni
Menai Bridge
Bangor
Rhoscolyn
link 10-11
Valley Airfield
A5
15
16
A55
Rhosneig
11
12.2
link 14-15
Bryn-siencyn
Port Dinorwic
Glasinfryn
Bethesda
12.1
Pentir
A5
Aberffraw
14
17
13
New-borough
Caernarfon
Bryn Bras
Llanddwyn
18
Dinas Dinlle
19
Bont-newydd
Glyn-llifon
Groeslon
Penygroes
LÔN EIFION CYCLEWAY
Aberdesach
20
Pant Glâs
Bryncir

N

0	km	8
0	mile	5

21

ABBREVIATIONS

There are only a few abbreviations on maps and in directions. They include

CTC	Cyclists' Touring Club
FC	Forestry Commission
GCC	Gwynedd County Council
NCR	National Cycle Route
NT	National Trust
NWWT	North Wales Wildlife Trust
OS	Ordnance Survey
RNLI	Royal National Lifeboat Institution
RSPB	Royal Society for the Protection of Birds
RUPP	Road Used as a Public Path
SSSI	Site of Special Scientific Interest
SUSTRANS	Sustainable Transport (charity)
WI	Women's Institute

BEAUMARIS TO MENAI BRIDGE AND TO PENMON

ROUTE   Ride 1: Beaumaris—Llanddona—Llansadwrn—
Butterfly Farm—Menai Bridge—Llandegfan—
Beaumaris
Ride 2: Beaumaris—Penmon—Trwyn Du—Penmon—
Llangoed—Llanfaes—Beaumaris

DISTANCE   Ride 1, 14 miles/22 km. Ride 2, 10 miles/16 km

ASCENT   Ride 1, 215 metres. Ride 2, 90 metres. A mixture of
level cycling, some climbs and a steep descent.

START   Beaumaris, Grid Ref 609765. The car park on the
green in front of the castle (pay in summer) or Menai
Bridge, Grid Ref 558721 (pay car park).

TO START   A5, A4080 to Menai Bridge, A545 from Menai Bridge
to Beaumaris.

These two routes give excellent cycling with some of the most spectacular views on the island. They are hilly in parts and best done by the inexperienced as two separate routes. I have described these two rides together, starting from Beaumaris as a figure of 8 shape. There are plenty of features of interest and many suitable places for picnic stops and exploring further on foot. There are several cafes in both towns. I have described an alternative way back from Llangoed to Beaumaris called Llanddona Loop. It is spectacular but hilly. It includes the only official bridleways in the whole of Anglesey but they are problematic! Short cuts would be possible (see OS map) for those who wish to avoid the towns. For a longer route: Ride 1 links with Ride 15 to Llangefni or via the bridge to Rides 16 or 17.

THE RIDES
RIDE 1 BEAUMARIS TO MENAI BRIDGE 14 miles
From the Green in **Beaumaris** cycle to the pier. Cross the road by the Bulkeley Arms Hotel, go under the archway and cross the High Street with

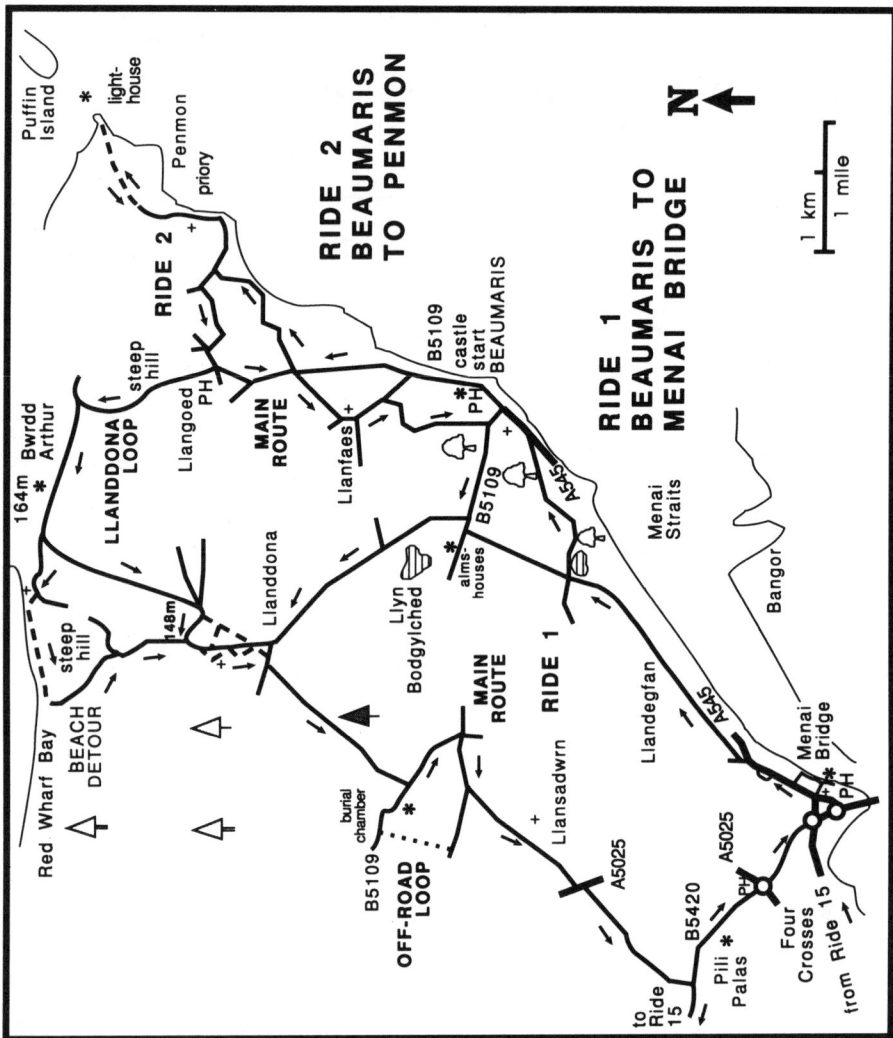

RIDE 2
BEAUMARIS
TO PENMON

RIDE 1
BEAUMARIS TO
MENAI BRIDGE

N

1 km
1 mile

Puffin Island *
light-house

Penmon priory

RIDE 2

164m Bwrdd Arthur *

steep hill

Llangoed PH

MAIN ROUTE

LLANDDONA LOOP

Llanddona

148m steep hill

Red Wharf Bay

BEACH DETOUR

B5109 OFF-ROAD LOOP

burial chamber *

Llansadwrn

A5025

B5420

Pili Palas *

to Ride 15

Four Crosses

from Ride 15

Menai Bridge PH *

A5025

Llandegfan

A5545

Menai Straits

Bangor

Llyn Bodgylched

alms-houses *

B5109

Llanfaes

castle start BEAUMARIS *PH

RIDE 1 MAIN ROUTE

24

care. There are plenty of amenities here. Leave the centre of town on the B5109 up the hill, passing several pubs and the church of St Mary.

It is about a mile of climbing. The route passes through the woods of Baron Hill (this has a derelict mansion dating from 1618) and under a pedestrian footbridge. At the first junction turn right by the gatehouse, **with care**, (or a 100 yard detour straight on and back to see the old almshouses 1613). After 100 yards is the boundary stone for Beaumaris/Llanfaes. Continue straight along this road for 2 miles to Llanddona. The Bulkeley Memorial is seen en route and then at the tiny hamlet of **Sling** is a house with miniature houses and windmill in its hummocky garden.

In **Llanddona** turn first left by the telephone, signed Wern y Wilan and Pentraeth. In ¼ mile turn first left signed Llansadwrn. It is 1½ miles, eventually passing the woods of Hafotty Covert and a converted chapel, on this lane with excellent views. At the main road decide on a slightly longer and hillier 2 mile route to pass a burial chamber, with about ½ mile on a track, or a shorter totally on road route through Llansadwrn village.

OFF-ROAD LOOP 2 miles *NB short walk included*
At the T-junction turn right, **with care**, onto the B5109 and there is a rapid descent round a bend. Don't go too fast or you will miss seeing the remains of an ancient burial chamber in a field on your left (not much of it survives!). Turn first left along a farm track (footpath) and **walk** straight on past the farm (Hendrefor) and at the lane turn left. It is a 1 mile climb along a pretty lane. At the T-junction turn right.

ROAD ROUTE 1 mile
Or at the T-junction turn left onto the B5109 and in ½ mile turn sharp right, **with care**. After ½ mile the Off-Road Loop route rejoins from the lane on the right.

MAIN ROUTE continued...
It is ½ mile into **Llansadwrn** where you pass the church (Eglwys Sadwrn Sant) dating from 500 AD. It has an elaborate cross (commemorating the fall in battle of Lt. McCorquodale at the battle of Spion Kop in South Africa in 1900 during the Boer War). Continue straight on for 1½ miles to the main road. This is a busy A road (the A5025) and **great care is needed** as you go straight across.

Follow this lane for 1¼ miles passing the refuse tip (Tomen Ysbwriel) which fortunately isn't too noticeable, apart from occasional smells. Be careful of heavy refuse vehicles and, at weekends, cars visiting the tip. At the end turn left onto the B5420 signed Bangor. There are good views of the Marquess of Anglesey's Column. After a mile is the Butterfly Farm, **Pili Palas**. Continue on for ¼ mile to the Four Crosses pub. Go straight across, **with great care,** and follow the B5402 into **Menai Bridge (alternative start)**, turning left at the next roundabout. There are two paying car parks here.

Turn left at the cross roads opposite the Bulkeley Arms in the town following signs for Beaumaris along the A545. There are cafes, shops and pubs here so all manner of refreshment stops are possible. There are also public toilets.

A detour straight across at the Bulkeley Arms to see the pier and slipway down Water Street is worthwhile as this also avoids the main road in the town. (If you want to see the suspension bridge continue down Water Street and along Beach Road. The Belgian promenade is past the bridge down a left fork.) Turn left by the Liverpool Arms into St George's Road/Ffordd Cynan. The entrance to St George's pier is immediately on the right. It is free at present. Then follow the minor road passing the Mostyn Arms, Marine Station and exit from the pier. Turn left at Menai Ville still in Ffordd Cynan. At the end turn right, **with care,** opposite the car park into the main road, Ffordd Cadnant, to Beaumaris.

Cadnant

After ¾ mile turn left along the old road over the Cadnant bridge: it is quieter and gives a better view of the stream and its estuary which usually has mallards feeding. Turn left, briefly back on the main road, and then first left steeply up the lane, signed Llandegfan. We now go more gently uphill. Go through **Llandegfan** passing scattered houses, a line of splendid beech trees, good viewpoints, a shop and a post office. Go straight on at the end of the village where the lane narrows. There is a bench with excellent views if you need a breather.

Take time to admire the wild flowers in the hedgebanks. In spring and early summer they are a delight with celandines, violets, Arum, stitchwort, wall pennywort and bedstraw. There is a very pleasant mile of lane passing through an unspoilt area of gorse and willow scrub often with birds to be seen at Llyn y Gors. After another ½ mile there is a cross roads. Beware, the sign here usually points the wrong way, maybe to keep motor traffic off the narrow steep lane, which of course we will take!

Turn right at this tiny cross roads, passing a shallow lake, and then the golf course. **TEST BRAKES NOW!** After a mile take **care** as the road drops very steeply (1 in 4) back to sea level in Beaumaris. Turn left with care onto the A545. Turn right, **with care**, to follow the coast past the pier and lifeboat station housing Blue Peter II and back to the car park.

Downhill into Beaumaris

RIDE 2 BEAUMARIS TO PENMON 10 miles

Go along the promenade towards the castle and pass the Beaumaris Marine World, follow the wall along the edge of the Green and turn right, **with care**, in front of the castle onto the B5109. It is a busy main road in summer and has double white lines in places. However there is a pavement alongside at first. It would be safer if children were allowed to use it.

After 1½ miles turn right, **with care**, signed Penmon at a small cross roads (the road on the left here is on our return route). Pass a large aerial and a nursing home. The road is undulating and passes a beech wood on the right and low-lying marshy fields on the left.

Keep right on the sharp bend, signed Penmon Priory and Point (the left turn, signed Penmon, is also on our return). There are more marshes often with plenty of birds and various breeds of cattle including Welsh blacks and Charolais. The narrow road follows the coast and has access to the shore at several places for picnic stops or exploring the beach. It soon reaches the **priory and dovecote**. Continue through past the pay kiosk (it is free for cyclists) into the privately owned Trwyn Du estate.

It is ¾ mile to the lighthouse and is a there-and-back ride on the same road. It is uphill for a short way and then a long gentle hill down to the sea. Beware, as there are a few deep potholes and a couple of speed ramps which can be unnerving if not unseating when taken at speed! It is a delightful ride with stupendous views of **Penmon lighthouse** and Puffin

Penmon lighthouse and Puffin Island

Island. There is a coastguard station and a cafe by the sea. Return by the same route to the priory and continue back along the coast, passing Black Rocks again, this time with views back up the Straits. Just past a bus shelter, on the bend signed Penmon, turn right, **with care.**

Go uphill on this narrow lane and turn first left marked Unsuitable for coaches/Anaddas i goets, by the house which was an old National School, dated AD 1851. Follow this undulating lane to its end. At the T-junction turn left and cycle downhill, **(or see Llanddona Loop)** crossing a small stream, into **Llangoed**. The road widens through the village. Continue straight on and pass the post office (which sells soft drinks and ices) and a little further opposite the Jerusalem Baptist Chapel is another shop. Towards the end of the village is a bus shelter (useful in case of bad weather).

At the first cross roads (seen on outward route) turn right, **with care**, signed

Llanfaes. Pass Kingsbridge caravan and camping and at the end turn left at the T-junction. After a very rapid ¼ mile descent is the beautiful church of **Llanfaes**. It is a few yards down the track on the left and is worth a detour. It is the church of St Catherine and has an elegant tall spire and amusing gargoyles. There is a huge ancient yew tree in the church yard. Return to the lane and turn left.

(**Alternatively** turn left and then immediately first right into a lane with a more gentle climb which follows a tiny stream. Pass Coed Bach woods which are good in early spring for wild garlic and wood anemones.)

Pass a small new housing estate also with a shop, and turn right, **with care**, signed Henllys Hall. Climb uphill (it really is worth it for the views) and at the top is the entrance to the hall. Bend left here where there is a wonderful view over Beaumaris, the castle, and the mountains of Snowdonia seen across the Straits. It is a lovely glide downhill for the end of the ride through the pleasant estate land with some magnificent old trees and grazing sheep.

At the T-junction turn left but beware of traffic while cycling through the town of **Beaumaris**. Pass the Sailors Return, the beautiful old church of St Mary's, the post office, shops, Bold Arms Hotel, and the George and Dragon all in quick succession going down to the High Street.

Dismount and cross over the main road, **with care**, and go under the archway. There are public toilets here as well as several cafes and the large Bulkeley Arms Hotel. Turn left by the pier and right with care along the track to the sea beside the lifeboat house. Follow the prom round, avoiding pedestrians and return to the car park on the Green.

LLANDDONA LOOP *NB very hilly*
Where the Main Route turns left towards Llangoed, turn right and immediately left, signed Llangoed Church etc on a well weathered wooden board. Pass the Board School dating from 1896, St Cawdraf's church then Capel MC Llangoed 1794. Climb up the straight *steep* hill. Near the top turn left signed Anaddas i gerbydau mawr (Unsuitable for long vehicles— tandems take note!). The lane goes gently down and up again. Notice the disused windmill on the hill to your left. At the grassy triangle turn right uphill. It is well worth it for the good views over the sea. Pass Ysgoldy Llanfihangel (MC) 1887. When you come round a bend the view to **Bwrdd Arthur** suddenly opens before you—it is impressive. The Bulkeley Memorial behind Beaumaris and even the distant mountains can be seen too.

At the foot of Bwrdd Arthur is a surfaced track leading round the hill. There is an isolated church reached by a short footpath through a field and views of the sea if you detour down here. There was an ancient hill fort here but nothing remains visible or accessible. After the bend continue onto the wider road.

(**Or for the beach** turn right and glide very steeply down for ½ mile. Turn right by the phone onto the bridleway along the top of the beach. You will find plenty of places for picnics. Pass the car park then climb steeply uphill. Turn right and enter Llanddona by the shop and pub.)

You will cycle close by the aerial—if it is a windy day the clouds scudding past the top of the aerial are amazing and make you realise how tall the aerial is. After almost a mile the road passes through an attractive heath with gorse, willow and heather. The bridleway, which leaves on the bend where two roads join on the left, supposedly follows the line of the pylons but at the time of writing is impenetrable. Continue round the bend and follow the road instead into the village of **Llanddona**. The way up from the beach rejoins here. There is a village store, a pub (the Owen Glyndwr) and a telephone. Turn left and cycle through the village.

The lane second on the right is a bridleway but is also disappointing. It is a road passing a chapel and scattered houses. Also near the end of the village the unsurfaced track on the left and then the right fork is an even bigger problem: it should lead to the other end of the bridleway over the heath but ends at the village football ground. Perhaps in the future they will be maintained to bridleway standard as they are the only bridleways on the island and Llanddona has plenty of horse riders. At the end of Llanddona either turn right to join Ride 1 to Menai Bridge or continue straight on for 1½ miles (following part of Ride 1 backwards) and turn left onto B5109 to return to Beaumaris (see Map).

OTHER INFORMATION

BEAUMARIS

Beaumaris was originally called Porth Wygyr, a Viking name. The name Beaumaris is Norman-French in origin, Beau Marais meaning beautiful marsh. The town was a short distance inland at Llanfaes. Here was the site of the court of Llewelyn the Great. The original Llanfaes Friary founded in 1237 was on the site of the Cammell Laird factory in private grounds (where Princess Joan and other great ladies of Gwynedd were buried). After the founding of the 'new town' of Beaumaris the local Welsh people were removed and resettled on the other side of the island at Rhosyr which was renamed Newborough. The present Henllys Hall, on the site of the court, is a country manor house built in 1853 by James Hansom, more famous for his design of the Hansom Cab. The house was auctioned in 1950 and bought by the Charity Commissioners who lent it to the Franciscan Friars. It was run as a school for monks until 1970 and became a hotel in 1971. Nowadays Beaumaris is famous for its fudge of many flavours! The sailing regatta takes place during the first two weeks of August.

The Castle is one of Edward's loveliest castles and is a World Heritage Listed Site. It was started in 1295 (but never finished) to control the Welsh. It was besieged and taken by Owain Glyn Dŵr's troops in 1403. In the Civil War parliamentary forces captured the castle in 1646. The walk round the walls is spectacular and there is a moat with swans and eels. There is a restored chapel and a crypt with an exhibition of Edward's castles. The concentric design can best be appreciated from above. It is open from March to October from 9.30-6.30 daily and in winter from 9.30-4 weekdays and 2-4 Sundays, tel 01248 810361.

The Gaol is situated on a back street. It was built in Victorian times as a model prison and survives remarkably intact: very realistic especially on a cold wet miserable day! **The courthouse** is near the castle and is open to the public when the court is not in session. It is probably the oldest courthouse still in use in Britain, tel 01248 810921.

The Museum of Childhood has a collection of toys, dolls, games and animated machines from the last 150 years to delight both the children and the adults. It also has some early cycles. It is privately owned by its founder Robert Brown who collected all the items and is for sale at present. It is found at 1, Castle Street and is open from Easter to end of October from 10.30-5.30 pm, Sunday noon-5pm (last admission 4.30 weekdays or 4 on Sundays), tel 01248 712498. There is an admission charge.

Beaumaris Marine World is a small centre with interesting aquarium displays. It is at the end of the prom and is open in summer. Adults £1.95, children £1 and family (2+3) £5. It also has an outdoor sea pool, cafe, Anglesey made ice cream, a gift shop and even a 60 foot worm which eats fish!

The Old Bulls Head The present pub dates from 1617 but was founded in 1472 as a posting inn. Charles Dickens and Samuel Johnson have both stayed here. It has the Beaumaris ducking stool and a water clock.

The Tudor Rose cafe is one of the oldest houses in Anglesey. It dates from 1400 and has been restored.

The George and Dragon dates from 1595 and is half timbered. It contains some original woodwork and a settle with the story of its namesakes depicted on it.

The Parish Church of St Mary and St Nicholas is well worth a visit. It houses the stone coffin of Princess Joan, wife of Llywelyn the Great and daughter of King John. She was buried at Llanfaes Friary originally founded in her honour but the coffin was moved to the church here in 1808. It rests in the south porch. In the door jamb on the north side is a deep socket for a thick timber beam which could be used to secure the church from attack. There is also an alabaster tomb of one of the Bulkeleys who died in 1490.

Pleasure Boat Trips on board Starida with commentary. 1 hour cruise to Penmon lighthouse and Puffin Island or down the Strait to Menai Bridge. Admission charge, tel 01248 810251.

PENMON
The Priory church of St Seiriol was founded in the 6th century. The church was rebuilt in the 12th century. The Celtic cross which used to be in the field is inside

Penmon Priory Church

the church. The remains of monastic buildings include a prior's house, a refectory and a dormitory. A short walk along a footpath on the left brings you to St Seiriol's cell cut into the cliff and the well where he used to baptise converts.

The Dovecote is amazingly well preserved considering that it dates from 1600. It has nearly 1000 pigeon holes.

The Lighthouse was built in 1837 and is automatic. It warns ships away from the dangerous rocks of Trwyn Du. Penmon has a pebble beach which is a favourite for geography and geology students but is not so good for bathing. The old lifeboat station nearby was functional from 1832 to 1915.

MENAI BRIDGE/PORTHAETHWY

Butterfly Farm Pili Palas (pili-pala means butterfly in Welsh so Pili Palas is a bilingual pun!) It has a wonderful collection of exotic butterflies and other mini-beasts. It is kept at sub-tropical temperatures to keep the exotic species happy and is also a good place for a cyclist to get warm on a cold day! Some of the creepy-crawlies are well displayed at child's eye level.

The Suspension Bridge is a classic design by Thomas Telford. The first stone was laid on 10th August 1819 and the bridge was opened to the public with great celebration on 30th Jan. 1826. It cost £120 000 to build. The original bridge had 16 chains each 1714 feet long from their fastenings in the rock on either side of the strait. The original roadways were only 12 feet wide. The suspending power of the chains was 2016 tons. Restoration work during the Second World War replaced the iron chains with steel ones. The only overtaking permitted is bikes by bikes! I think it is the most graceful design of bridge in Britain—if not the whole world!

The Art Gallery/Oriel Tegfryn is on the outskirts of the town. It houses exhibitions of paintings mainly by local artists.

The Fair/Ffair y Borth dates at least from 1691 and was traditionally a horse and livestock market. It is held annually on 24th October (or 23rd if 24th is a Sunday). It no longer has the farm animals but does have all the fun of a fair and busy street market. It is a very lively and popular event and the whole town is taken over by it.

St George's Pier used to be a large traditional wooden affair. From here ships exported slate and imported timber. It used to be possible to catch a steamer to Liverpool from here. The large timber yard is still on the same site here but is due to move soon. The pier is mainly used nowadays by the University's marine research vessel the Prince Madog as well as being popular with the local fishermen.

The Belgian Promenade Passing the remnants of the old open air swimming pool brings you to the Belgian Promenade. This was built as a 'thank you' gesture to the townspeople for looking after Belgian refugees during the war. It is fun to cycle along here passing the old paddling pool and Coed Cyrnol to **Church Island** especially twice a year on the equinoctial high tides when the prom is flooded (NB the seawater doesn't do the chain any good). The church is dedicated to Saint Tysilio and dates from AD 630. Roman coins have been found in the wood, Coed Cyrnol.

There are excellent views down the strait to **Stevenson's Railway Bridge**. Since the reconstruction it is unique in Britain carrying a road (the A5) on an upper deck. The accidentally started fire was an awesome sight to watch with flaming tarry timbers falling and sizzling in the water below. Beside Church Island is the remains of an old fish weir and there is good bird watching in the bay with plenty of shelduck, herons, cormorants and waders to see. Incredibly strong and complex currents run in the strait between the bridges reaching 8 knots at spring highs. In the past I have enjoyed sailing in most parts of the Menai Strait but the infamous whirlpools known as the **Swellies** are best avoided. The sights and sounds of the water here are ever-changing and the same view is never boring. It must rank amongst other famous stretches of water like the Minches for its challenging wild nature and spectacular beauty. It is one of my favourite places.

THE PUBS

The Sailors Return (Boddingtons), the half timbered Bold Arms Hotel (1892) (Burtonwood), George and Dragon (1410) (Robinsons) are all in Beaumaris and serve bar meals, as do the Bulkeley Arms Hotel, the Old Bulls Head (1595) and the Liverpool Arms.

The Four Crosses and the Bulkeley Arms (both Robinsons), the Auckland Arms and the Liverpool Arms—recommended—(both Greenalls) are all in Menai Bridge and serve bar meals. The Mostyn Arms by the pier is also Greenalls.

Owen Glyndwr (Youngers) is in Llanddona and serves bar food.

RED WHARF BAY TO LLYN CEFNI

ROUTE	Red Wharf Bay—Brynteg—Tregaian—Llyn Cefni—Llanbedrgoch—Red Wharf Bay
DISTANCE	15 miles/24 km. Short Cut 7 miles. Extra mile by lake
ASCENT	140 metres. One climb up from Red Wharf Bay and some undulating lanes.
START	Red Wharf Bay. Public car park by sea, in front of Ship Inn, Grid Ref 530812. Or, Llyn Cefni car park on B5111, Grid Ref 452783.
TO START	A5025 from Menai Bridge. Turn right 1½ miles past Pentraeth to Traeth Coch. Or, from Llangefni take the B5110 and then the B5111 for 2 miles to Llyn Cefni.

Really delightful quiet inland lanes and extensive views of Red Wharf Bay are the highlights of this outing. We go from the sea to the lake, Llyn Cefni, or vice versa by starting at the tiny park by the lake. There is ¼ mile of off-road near the start and you might be able to do a short there-and-back off-road along the forest track beside Llyn Cefni. The route interlinks with Ride 4 (Moelfre) and also at the lake with Ride 15 (Llanfairpwll) so longer routes and variations are easily arranged.

One is really spoilt for choice of good cycling lanes in the Benllech 'hinterland'. These two routes are ideal for all the caravanning and camping sites in this area. We have done so many permutations that it was difficult unscrambling them but I think we have worked out the best routes! Residents of Benllech should join the route via Tynygongl and the B5108 (see map). The short cut gives a short ride of 7 miles for the very young or for emergencies. It uses a delightful lane back from Brynteg to Llanbedrgoch.

THE RIDE

MAIN ROUTE 15 miles
From Red Wharf Bay, go up the steep hill for only 100 yards, passing St David's Estate entrance.

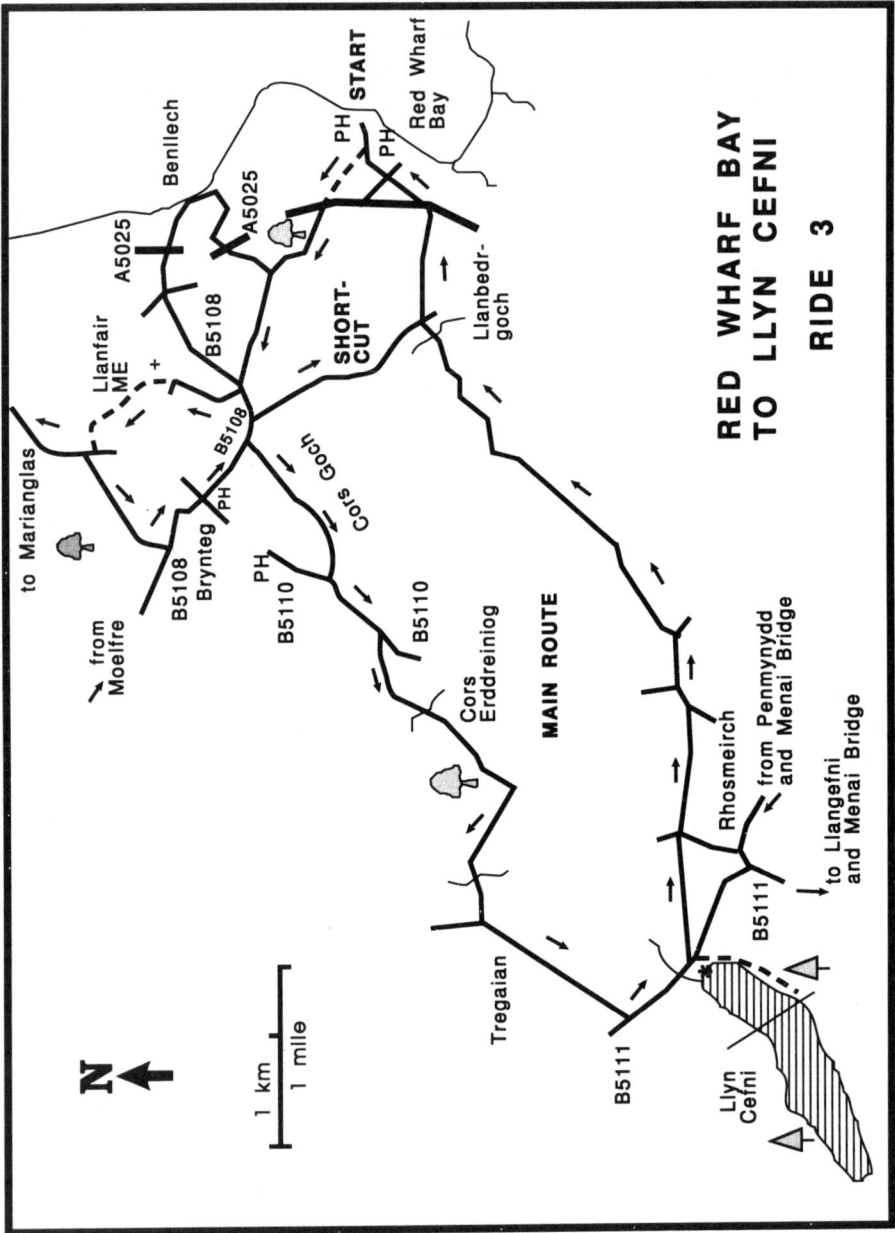

RED WHARF BAY
TO LLYN CEFNI

RIDE 3

START

Red Wharf Bay

Benllech

A5025

A5025

B5108

Llanfair ME

to Marianglas

from Moelfre

B5108

Brynteg

PH

B5108

Cors Goch

SHORT-CUT

Llanbedr-goch

PH

B5110

B5110

Cors Erddreiniog

MAIN ROUTE

Tregaian

Rhosmeirch

from Penmynydd
and Menai Bridge

to Llangefni
and Menai Bridge

B5111

B5111

Llyn Cefni

N

1 km
1 mile

OFF-ROAD ROUTE ½ mile
Turn next right along a track with tarmac at first (signed private road to farm and footpath). Where it bends right to the farm keep straight on. It is now unsurfaced and goes up first and then steeply down to the main road. Turn right, **with care**, onto the A5025.

ROAD ROUTE ¾ mile
Alternatively to stay on road, keep on for ¼ mile and turn right and right again at the T-junction with the A5025. Follow this for ¼ mile to the first left turn.

MAIN ROUTE continued...
Turn immediately left into a narrow lane (Ffordd gûl). The Old Station House on the left is a reminder of the old railway which used to cross here. There is a bench on the right if you need a rest already! Remnants of old woodland are found here with ash, elder, sycamore, beech, hazel and rose. In spring there is a profusion of wild flowers with rock rose, black medick, herb bennet, bird's foot trefoil, speedwell, herb robert, pink campion, hedge parsley, enchanter's nightshade, ramsons, bryony and goosegrass and mother-in-law's tongue fern—to name but a few!

It is a pleasant lane for over a mile. Pass bungalows and an old mill cottage (Ty y Felin), a field perhaps with ponies grazing, then a quarry, and a field with sheep. The walls here are covered with pennywort. Pass the Pacemaker Leisure Centre and Bwlch caravan park. At the end turn left onto the B5108 and immediately right by the chapel signed Eglwys Llanfair ME. There is a width restriction of *6 ymhen ½ milltir* ahead—be warned those cyclists wider than 6 ymhens!

Go up the narrow lane; a small lake is visible down to the left behind Tyddyn Sargent. The hawthorn hedges are almost invisible behind their ivy drapery. There are also sloe bushes and a field (sometimes with donkeys) to the right. At the fork bear right and immediately pass Eglwys Santes Fair (St Mary's) at Llanfair Mathafarn Eithaf. It is an attractive tiny church with a single bell.

Go straight on at the 6 foot width restriction and immediately at the bend bear right (dead end to the left). The very narrow lane goes downhill and then up again. At first it is like a tunnel with overhanging hazel, hawthorn and bramble. On emerging it passes lovely flower meadows, old cottages and farms on hummocky ground. Ignore a tiny right turn and go down to the main road, the B5110 (just outside Marianglas). Turn right, **with care**, and pass the low cottages of Pwll Farm.

Turn first sharp left, signed Pen Parc. After the previous deep lanes the

Eglwys Santes Fair

views now start to open up as we ride across a limestone plateau with wide sheep pastures bounded by long white limestone walls. There are isolated copses of trees but this tends to be a breezy area. We climb gently past Pen Parc camping and caravanning park and up to the brow. After ½ mile at the T-junction turn left towards Brynteg. This ¼ mile is in common with the Moelfre Ride. Pass the post office in the village of **Bryn Teg**. At the cross roads by the California go straight across, **with care**, onto the B5108. After ½ mile turn first right or **see Short Cut**.

SHORT CUT BACK TO RED WHARF BAY 7 miles in total
After a further ¼ mile on the B5108 take the second right and follow a quiet attractive lane for just over a mile to Llanbedrgoch. Rejoin the Main Route at * below by turning left at the post office.

MAIN ROUTE continued...
Follow Lôn Bryn Mair, passing several camping and caravanning sites, eg Glan Gors. It is a varied and interesting lane with views to the left initially of Cors Goch—Anglesey's biggest bog! There are scattered houses, small woods and pastures. Look out for a mixture of farm animals: you may see carthorses, beef and dairy cattle, highland cattle, goats, geese, cocks, hens and even the odd donkey!

After a mile at the T-junction turn left onto the B5110. After ½ mile turn first right, **with care,** just after Nant Newydd Quarry, into a narrow lane. Pass a bog called Cors Erddreiniog and go under the huge pylon line. Go round a bend by a large farm with relict ash woodlands and a noisy rookery. It is over a mile to the end of the lane. Cross a small stream which feeds Llyn Cefni. At the T-junction turn right into another narrow lane.

After 200 yards turn left at the T-junction onto a wider road. Pass a large old farm and next to it the church of St Caian, with a single bell, in the tiny hamlet of **Tregaian.** It is gently downhill on this good road so faster speeds are now possible! It is a mile to the end with views of the distant mountains. Turn left onto the B5111.

It is only ½ mile down to Llyn Cefni: you will have glimpses of the lake sheltered by the forest ahead. Cross the stream at the bottom of the valley, pass the onward route down the lane on the left and climb up for a few yards to turn right, **with care,** into the picnic area and small car park for the reservoir. You are now 10½ miles from the start—time for a picnic perhaps! The track straight on is only for the 'rough-stuff' enthusiast: it is cyclable for about ½ mile there and back. (A detour on foot first right on a short footpath leads down to the bird hide.)

From **Llyn Cefni (alternative start)** turn left out of the car park onto the B5111 and immediately first right, **with care,** into a narrow lane with interesting hedges. This lane is in common with the Ride 15 for ½ mile but in the opposite direction. Go up to the crest of a hillock and straight across the minor cross roads. There are good views of the mountains of Snowdonia. At the T-junction turn left onto the B5110 and first right, signed Talwrn and Pentraeth, 7.5 tons. Go under the pylons, past greenhouses and up hill for ¼ mile. Turn first left and in 200 yards is Bwrth y Felin, Granary Cottage and a converted windmill (without sails).

There is a narrow wood at first and then a lovely long lane with views of the mountains followed by views ahead to Red Wharf Bay. Go downhill and into a hollow by a shady wooded stream valley by Bryn Du and Ty Pwyll. After 2¼ miles you will reach **Llanbedrgoch.** The post office in Llanbedrgoch is on the left and sells ice creams and soft drinks etc. At the staggered junction go across, following the sign for Traeth Coch. There is a bench for a quick rest! * **The Short Cut rejoins here.**

MAIN ROUTE continued...
Go through the village (dim palmant/no footway) and down the hill. Follow the winding lane round several bends and cross a long since disused railway. Turn left onto the A5025 and first right, **WITH EXTREME CARE,** signed Traeth Coch. Go straight on past the shop and the Bryn Tirion Hotel

and steeply downhill back to the start at **Red Wharf Bay**. (Or to continue the ride, if you started somewhere else and want to avoid a climb, you could turn left by the Bryn Tirion but this would omit the beach.)

The Ship Inn

OTHER INFORMATION

RED WHARF BAY/TRAETH COCH

The beach is an impressive 5 miles long. Unless you are very familiar with the sandbanks and channels it is wisest not to venture far out onto the sands during the incoming tide! There is a pleasant walk beyond the hotels round the headland past Castell Mawr. This is a massive cliff of limestone and probably the site of an early British fortress.

LLYN CEFNI

This is Anglesey's second biggest lake and is stocked with rainbow trout. In winter the visiting birds include swans—both mute and whooper; ducks—ruddy, widgeon, teal, mallard, tufted, pochard and goldeneye; and other species—coot, moorhen, little and great crested grebe and woodcock. In summer visitors include: grey wagtail, sedge warbler, willow warbler, whitethroat, blackcap, chiffchaff, tits, treecreeper, great spotted woodpecker, siskin, redpoll, crossbill, bullfinch and jay.

There are a couple of picnic tables and some amenity planting of a variety of trees, eg fir, larch, spruce and a few deciduous trees, around a small car park. It makes an ideal spot for a picnic. Those with energy to spare can ride safely away from traffic along the cart track for a little way, but it is rather muddy, and where it has been mended with limestone chippings it is bumpy! If visiting the bird hide quietness pays off if you want to watch the birds.

TREGAIAN

The name seems to have 3 possible spellings: Tregaian, Tregaean and Tregayan! There is a story of a man who lived here and died at the ripe old age of 105 in 1581. He had 22 children by his first wife, 10 by his second and 4 by his third, not to mention another 7 out of wedlock! When his youngest son was born his eldest was 81! I wonder if this is a record? Such prolific families seem to have died out now as the hamlet is very tiny but the church remains to show that the congregation must have been much larger in the past.

THE PUBS

The Ship Inn (free house) (recommended) and Min y Don (Bass) are both at Red Wharf Bay and do bar meals.
The California is at Brynteg but is often closed.
Bryn Tirion Hotel is at Red Wharf Bay.
Old Boathouse Cafe is at Red Wharf Bay.

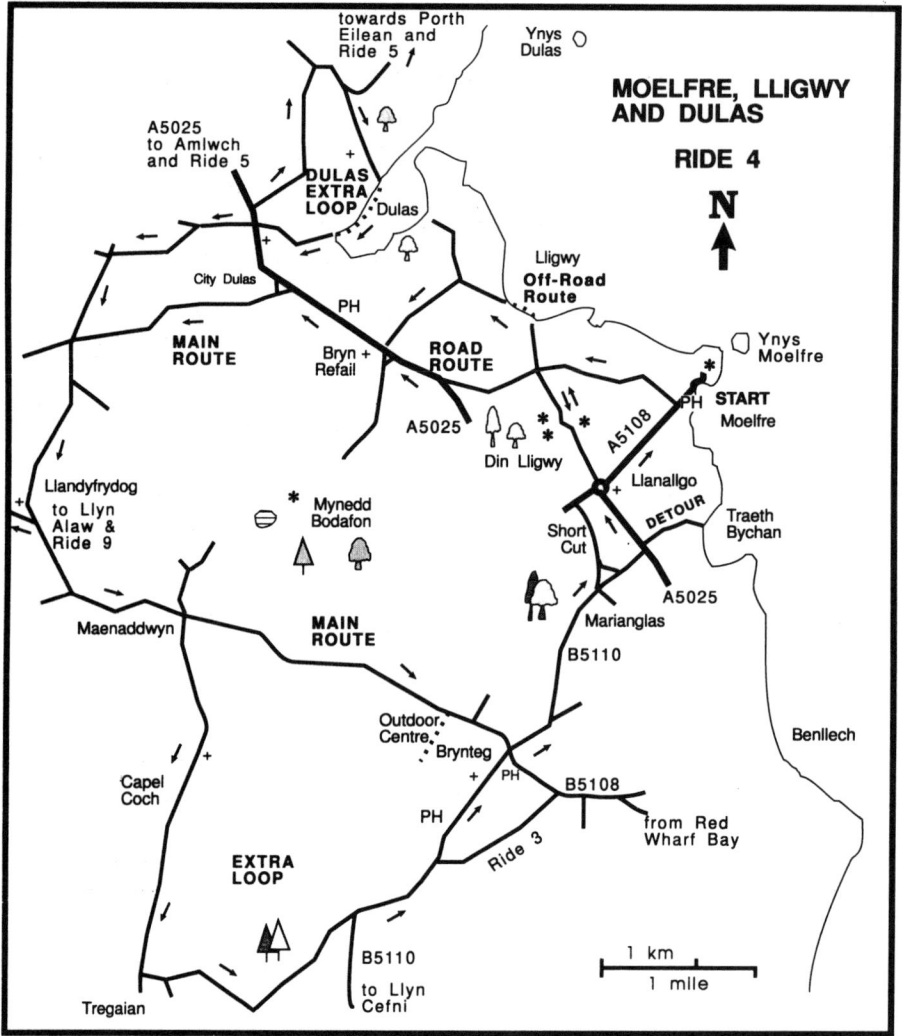

MOELFRE, LLIGWY
AND DULAS

RIDE 4

N

towards Porth
Eilean and
Ride 5

Ynys
Dulas

A5025
to Amlwch
and Ride 5

DULAS
EXTRA
LOOP

Dulas

City Dulas

PH

MAIN
ROUTE

Bryn
Refail

A5025

Lligwy
Off-Road
Route

ROAD
ROUTE

Ynys
Moelfre

PH START

Moelfre

Din Lligwy

Llanallgo

A5108

DETOUR

Traeth
Bychan

Llandyfrydog
to Llyn
Alaw &
Ride 9

Mynedd
Bodafon

Short
Cut

A5025

Maenaddwyn

MAIN
ROUTE

Marianglas

B5110

Benllech

Outdoor
Centre

Brynteg

PH

B5108

Capel
Coch

PH

Ride 3

from Red
Wharf Bay

EXTRA
LOOP

1 km

1 mile

Tregaian

B5110
to Llyn
Cefni

RIDE 4

MOELFRE, LLIGWY AND DULAS

ROUTE	Moelfre—Lligwy—City Dulas (+ Dulas Extra Loop)— Llandyfrydog—Maenaddwyn (+ Extra Loop)— Brynteg— Marianglas (+ Traeth Bychan Detour)— Llanallgo—Moelfre
DISTANCE	13 miles/21 km + Extra Loops of 4½, 3, and ¾ miles
ASCENT	205 metres. Rather hilly.
START	Moelfre public car park, Grid Ref 512863.
TO START	A5025 from Menai Bridge via Benllech, then right at roundabout on A5108 to Moelfre. Left by bus stop signed toilet, left into Ffordd Lligwy and left into car park (free and toilets).

From sea level we eventually reach the dizzy height of 99 metres at Maenaddwyn and have a look at Mynydd Bodafon without climbing all of it! The route involves a short walk across the superb Lligwy beach for the 'holiday' cyclist but there is a road alternative. At Lligwy there is a car park and snack bar, and several caravan parks. Those staying at one of the caravan parks can join the route direct. There are links with Ride 3 so anyone wanting a longer route could link the two together or do various permutations of the lanes.

There are three extra loops to choose from. The one to Dulas is for those wishing to visit this huge unspoilt beach; it involves some off-road. The one from Maenaddwyn is for those wanting a longer ride; it doesn't have any particular place of interest, just quiet lanes. The one to Traeth Bychan is a there-and-back to visit this popular sailing cove. For refreshments, as well as the pubs, there are cafes or kiosks at Moelfre, Lligwy and Traeth Bychan.

THE RIDE

MAIN ROUTE 13 miles
MOELFRE TO LLIGWY
Either at the beginning or end of the ride it is worth visiting the cove and Seawatch Centre despite the hill! It is described here first.

From the public car park in **Moelfre** come out by the bollards by the toilets and turn left steeply down the short hill to visit the cove first before the ride. Pass the Old Ship's Bell and Ann's Pantry tea room and shop. Overlooking the sea is the Kinmel Arms. There is a small paying car park (usually full) and a small beach shop. There is a bench beside the water which is ideal for a picnic spot. It is worth leaving the bikes secured and going for a short stroll along to the life boat station along the footpath by the sea. There are good views of Ynys Moelfre (Moelfre Island) and the bay. To visit the Seawatch Centre ride on up the hill. It is only a few yards on the right.

Return back down the hill to the cove and then up the hill to the bus stop and turn right. The road soon leaves the houses as it climbs gently and becomes a delightful lane with extensive views over the sea. It is a mile to the cross roads above Lligwy. (**The Short Cut** omitting Moelfre rejoins here.) A short ½ mile detour to visit **Din Lligwy, Burial Chamber and Hen Capel**

A hut circle at Din Lligwy

Lligwy is a must. Turn left up the lane and then return to this cross roads after your archaeological exploits. Also decide here whether you wish to omit Lligwy beach and stay on road or continue on the Main Route over the sand.

ROAD ROUTE omitting Lligwy beach
Turn left after the detour to the ancient monuments and in 1 mile at the

main road turn right, **with care,** and continue to rejoin the route at Bryn Refail.

MAIN ROUTE continued...
LLIGWY TO CITY DULAS
A glide downhill for ½ mile brings you swiftly to the big car park (another possible start) with shop and snack bar (open in summer) and public toilets. Go down onto **Traeth Lligwy** by the concrete ramp behind the shop. Walk (cycling is not easy—avoid getting sand in any moving parts—teeth especially!) across the beach towards the river. Cross the streams by wooden and stone bridges. Cycle through another car park and then prepare for a climb! Turn left at the first junction (straight on would give a short there-and-back detour to see the south shore of Dulas Bay but be warned: you would need to drop downhill to see the sea and then climb back up again.) Pass Tyddyn Isaf and Capel Elen caravan parks.

Brynrefail

After ¾ mile at Bryn Refail Craft Shop turn right onto the A5025, **with care,** and follow the main road for ¾ mile. It is steeply downhill. At the bottom turn left before the coalyard at **City Dulas OR see Dulas Extra Loop)** and cross the Afon Goch by a very old bridge. City Dulas is a very small hamlet!

DULAS EXTRA LOOP extra 4½ miles (+ a climb) and **LINK TO RIDE 5**
NB NOT SUITABLE FOR CHILDREN
Continue on the main road for another ½ mile and turn right, **with care,** on
the brow of the hill, signed Llys Dulas. Follow this lovely narrow lane for
over a mile gently uphill to a T-junction and turn right, signed Llaneilian
Church. After ¼ mile take the first right fork **or See Link from Ride 4 to 5.**
It is now downhill all the way to the beach but it is worth a brief pause to
look at the church of Llanwenllwyfol with its slender stone spire. At the
bottom of the hill the tarmac ends at the beach where you are advised to
walk!

The wide expanse of **Dulas Beach**/Traeth Dulas lies before you—ideal for
picnics. Turn right and follow the track across the top of the shore for ½
mile to the narrow road where the tarmac starts again. Climb uphill for ¾
mile to Llaneuddog.

Traeth Dulas

Go straight across the main road, **with care,** into a narrow lane. After ½
mile take the left fork in the woods. There is a good view of Parys
Mountain. After ½ mile at the cross roads turn left. After ½ mile reach Capel
Parc and rejoin the Main route at + by going straight across the minor cross
roads.

LINK FROM RIDE 4 TO 5 2½ miles
Instead of going down to Dulas beach, fork left signed Llaneilian. It is a
narrow undulating lane with high banks covered in wild flowers and ferns.

Pass the private entrance to Llys Dulas. Climb up through the deciduous woods where you may well see pheasants before Christmas-time! Keep left at the minor T-junction signed Llaneilian (right is to the disused church and Bryn Fuches only). The lane is now grassy down the centre and muddy. The aerials on Mynedd Eilian soar ahead. It is a wild and remote corner of the island. There are sheep pastures and rocky knolls. Keep straight on signed 'bends for 2 miles'! Pass an old look-out point. The road surface soon improves. Down to the right are the steep cliffs covered with gorse bordering Freshwater Bay. Go steeply downhill to cross the stream feeding the Bay. Climb up passing a few scattered cottages.

There is a marvellous panorama over the sea towards Llaneilian, Point Lynas and the headlands at Amlwch from this road as we contour round the hill on a narrow ledge. Go straight on and downhill through the hamlet of Pengorffwysfa. At the T-junction turn right by the telephone and bus shelter and immediately sharp right again. Continue downhill towards Point Lynas and check your brakes as the steep section is next! At the bottom of the hill cross a tiny stream and then, at the junction, to visit Porth Eilian turn right, or to continue onto Ride 5 turn left.

MAIN ROUTE continued...
DULAS TO MAENADDWYN
It is 1½ miles along the undulating lane from City Dulas, passing marshy ground with the brilliant yellow flag iris, in the valley of the Afon Goch.

+ **(Dulas Loop Rejoins)** At the cross roads at Capel Parc, by the post office, turn left signed Llangefni. After ¼ mile keep straight on and cross a stream. This area provides a good opportunity to admire the hedgerow flowers such as scabious, clover, stitchwort, meadow buttercup, wall pennywort, campion, foxglove, purple vetch, forget-me-not, violet and blue geranium. After ¾ mile cross under the pylons and then over a stream and pass the church in the tiny hamlet of **Llandyfrydog**.

After ¼ mile turn left at a T-junction signed Benllech and Llangefni. In ½ mile turn left again at Clorach Bach (by Carreg Leidr standing stone) and then cross the Afon Goch. There is a gentle climb uphill for ¾ mile, going diagonally across the shoulder of Mynydd Bodafon. Then at **Maenaddwyn** cross roads the highest point of the ride is reached at 99 metres. Decide on the Extra Loop or continue the Main Loop.

EXTRA LOOP 3 miles further
At Maenaddwyn turn immediately right by the post office, signed Llangefni. In just over 1 mile pass the old windmill at Capel Coch. After another mile along this quiet lane turn left at a post box on a right hand bend. (The next

couple of miles is in common with part of Ride 3 but in the opposite direction.) In ¼ mile turn left and pass remnants of old woodland, pastures full of buttercups and some early purple orchids at the right time of year and a hazel hedge with climbing bryony. It is briefly uphill and then there is a babbling brook (in Gors Erddreiniog) with wild garlic and horsetails.

At the B5110 turn left, pass Nant Newydd quarry and a caravan park. After ½ mile turn right opposite a cypress enclosed field. There is a cluster of old houses then a field containing a varied collection of animals—possibly! Pass Glan Gors caravan park and then turn left onto the B5108 on the outskirts of **Brynteg**. It is ½ mile to the cross roads in Brynteg to rejoin the Main Route by turning right onto the B5110 at ** below.

MAIN ROUTE continued...
MAENADDWYN TO MARIANGLAS
At Maenaddwyn continue straight on, signed Benllech and Llanerchymedd, for 2¼ miles on a pleasant quiet lane. It is mainly downhill. Cross the tiny stream—the Afon Lligwy. It is near here that the scenery makes a subtle change as we pass from the hard rocks of the rugged north of the island to the limestone of the south. There is an old limestone quarry on the right and more wild flowers and attractive dry stone walls. Pass Tyddin Philip (Activity Centre) and Min-y-Ffrwd caravan park and enter Brynteg. At the cross roads by the California pub in **Brynteg** turn left. ** **(Extra Loop rejoins)**

Follow the B5110 for 1¼ miles, passing The Lodge caravan park and the road to Llaneugrad parish church. Pass the Parciau Arms pub and the Pigeon Loft caravan park just before **Marianglas**.

In Marianglas there is a general store, telephone, antique shop, closed bakery and huge village green with a stone cross and handy bench. It is better to follow the lane round the back of the green past Bryn Hafod stores and the post office. Go down to the main road A5025 and turn left, signed Amlwch. (OR See Detour to Traeth Bychan.)

DETOUR TO TRAETH BYCHAN extra ¾ mile
Go across the A5025, **with care**, down the lane for just over ¼ mile. It is a glide all the way downhill to the sea at Traeth Bychan. There is a car park with toilets and a beach shop/snack bar open in the summer. There is a very active sailing club here and a caravan park so this narrow lane can be busy during the summer holidays and best avoided then. It is quite a pull back up hill retracing your route to the main road where it is necessary to turn right, **with extreme care.**

MAIN ROUTE continued...
MARIANGLAS TO MOELFRE
Follow the A5025 for only ½ mile. The pavement is fairly wide and it would be safer if children were allowed to use this. Pass Canolfan Llanallgo on the left. At the roundabout turn right, **with extreme care**, to Moelfre on the A5108 passing Llanallgo chapel, the track to Oak Lodge Hotel (restaurant meals) and a little further down the hill a fish and chip shop. The left turning to the public car park is next on the left **(recommended Start)**.

SHORT CUT past Lligwy Ancient Monuments omitting Moelfre
Turn left behind the green at Marianglas. Keep left on the bend and cycle ½ mile to the main road at **Llanallgo**. Turn right, **with care**, onto the A5025 and follow it with care for ½ mile to the roundabout. (There is a pavement on the left and it would be safer if children could use this.) Turn left signed Lligwy. It is a mile along this lane with extensive sea views. Pass the burial chamber, Din Lligwy and Hen Capel. At the cross roads go straight across towards Lligwy beach to rejoin the Main Route.

OTHER INFORMATION
LLIGWY
Lligwy comes from Llug, meaning gleaming bright or flashing—an apt name when the sun shines on the clean water here. Alternatively it might come from Lugos, a

Hen Capel

Celtic deity. Hen Capel (the old chapel) dates from various periods in the 12th, 14th and 16th century and has a crypt. Just beyond the hazel wood is a polygonal, walled, defended village built during the Roman period and mainly occupied in the

4th century. There are also round and rectangular huts. In the field near the top of the hill is Lligwy Burial Chamber which dates from the end of the Neolithic period, 2500-2000 BC. It was used for communal burials and was originally covered with a mound of earth and stones.

MOELFRE

Moelfre was a traditional fishing village and still retains much of its old character as, having a pebbly beach, it doesn't get too busy. The cove gives a safe anchorage to yachts. Ynys Moelfre abounds with gulls and other seabirds. Porpoises have been sighted in the bay.

The lifeboat was established in 1830. One of the most famous wrecks here was that of the sailing ship the Royal Charter which was driven onto the rocks in a great storm in 1859. She was returning from Australia to Liverpool so it is ironic that having come so far she foundered so near to home. 452 lives were lost. Exactly 100 years later was another shipwreck, that of the Hindlea, when 8 crew members were rescued by the Moelfre lifeboat. The submarine Thetis grounded off Traeth Bychan in 1939 after disastrous trials and her crew were drowned. She was later refitted and renamed the Thunderbolt. Traeth Bychan is now the home of The Red Wharf Bay Sailing Club and has been very popular for dinghy sailing since the 1960s.

The Seawatch Centre opened in 1994 and is run by Anglesey Coastal Heritage. Here you can find out about the rescues made by the lifeboats and their courageous crews and about the famous shipwrecks in the area. You can go on board a real lifeboat, the Bird's Eye. There is information on maritime history, marine ecology, weather forecasting, tides and navigation, as well as a remote controlled camera to watch ships and birds. The Centre is open from April 1 to Sept 30, Tuesday to Saturday and Bank Holiday Mondays from 11-5, tel 01407 840845/6 or Warden tel 01248 410277. It has a small RNLI shop.

TRAETH DULAS

The name Afon Dulas means blue black stream (like the river Douglas in England). This is an enormous unspoiled beach and is one of the least visited on the island. It is estuarine and almost landlocked with interesting salt marsh development on the north and wooded banks on the south side. Don't be tempted to cross from side to side—there is a big river in the way! You can just see the tower on Ynys Dulas over the headland. This tiny island is visited by seals. The tower was put there in the last century as a beacon to warn shipping away from the rocks.

The church of Llanwenllwyfo at Dulas was built in 1856 to replace a ruined one near Llysdulas manor house. It apparently contains an interesting font, oak screen and brass from the old church as well as 15th and 16th century Flemish glass.

MYNYDD BODAFON

This is only 178 metres high and so is hardly a mountain! It does have a minor road over it but we haven't used it as there seems to be enough climbing already on this route! There used to be a signal station on the summit. Beacons were lit to warn the local population of invaders from the sea. On the SW side are remains of ancient hut circles called **Cwtiau'r Gwyddelod.**

THE PUBS

Kinmel Arms in Moelfre (Robinsons) serves bar meals. It has picnic tables outside overlooking the sea.

The Pilot Boat (Robinsons) on the right hand side of the main road between Lligwy and Dulas

The California (Ansells) is at Brynteg and has a small beer garden but is often closed.

Parciau Arms (free house, real ale) in Marianglas serves bar meals till 9.30.

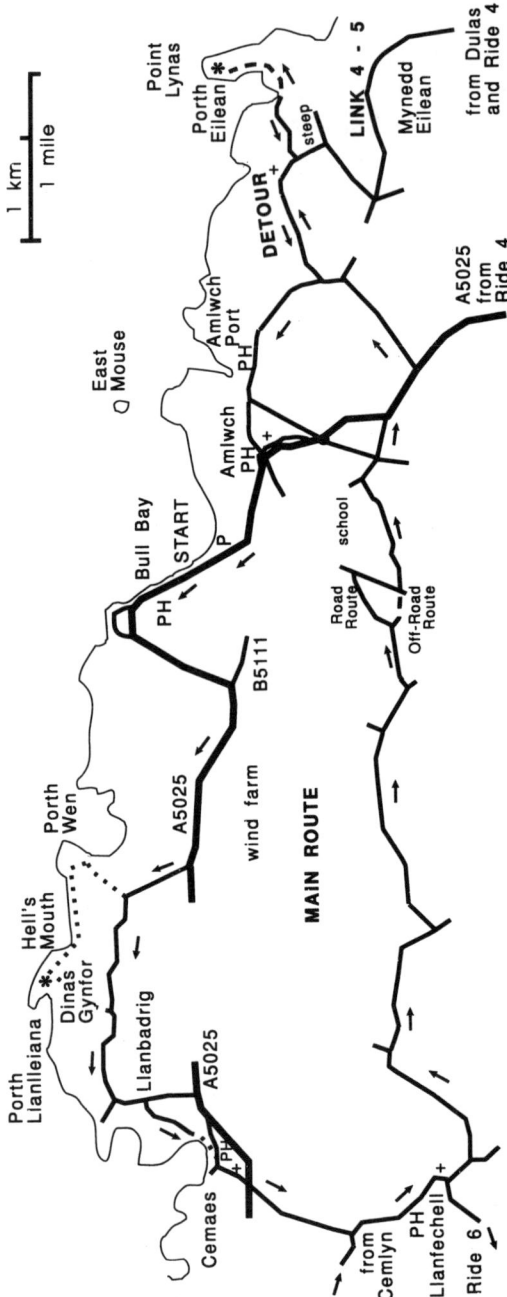

CEMAES, BULL BAY AND AMLWCH

RIDE 5

N

1 km
1 mile

Middle Mouse

Porth Llanlleiana

Hell's Mouth

Dinas Gynfor

Porth Wen

East Mouse

Bull Bay

PH

START

P

A5025

B5111

wind farm

MAIN ROUTE

Llanbadrig

A5025

Cemaes
+ PH

from Cemlyn

PH
Llanfechell

Ride 6

Road Route

Off-Road Route

school

Amlwch
PH
+

Amlwch
Port
PH

DETOUR
+

steep

Porth Eilean

Point Lynas

LINK 4 - 5

Mynedd Eilean

from Dulas
and Ride 4

A5025
from
Ride 4

52

RIDE 5

CEMAES, BULL BAY AND AMLWCH

ROUTE	Bull Bay—Cemaes Bay—Llanfechell—Llaneilian—Amlwch—Bull Bay
DISTANCE	15½ miles/25 km. Llaneilian detour 2 miles each way
ASCENT	160 metres Hilly!
START	Bull Bay. Small car park by sea, opposite golf club entrance, Grid Ref 430938.
TO START	On the A5025 about a mile from Amlwch.

This is a very varied route including seaside, cliffs, coves, inland rural lanes, villages, and a modern wind farm. There are some hills, one roundabout and a few right turns onto main roads but they are usually quiet. It is the most northerly ride we do. It has a rugged landscape with wide open sea views but can be rather windy on the exposed sections. You can shorten the route by omitting Llaneilian, or lengthen it at Llanfechell where it joins with Ride 6 or at Llaneilian by the link to Ride 4. Allow 3 hours at a slow pace.

THE RIDE

MAIN ROUTE 15½ miles

Turn right, **with care**, and cycle down the A5025 into **Bull Bay**. Pass the Trecastell Hotel. Turn right, **with care**, signed toilet, then keep left down to the bay. There are picnic benches by the shingly beach. The Bull Bay Hotel is to the right. Pass a telephone and toilets. The wooded embankment abounds with wild flowers, bluebell, celandine, stitchwort and kingcups. It is uphill to the T-junction where you turn right, **with care**, onto the main road.

There is a pavement at first. It is 2 miles, with views of the wind farm, to a post box and layby on the right. Turn right, **with care**, just before these. It is a pleasant narrow lane ablaze with gorse flowers almost all year round. On the bend two footpaths leave to the right. The second one is a track which makes a good diversion on foot to see Porth Wen and the industrial archaeology of derelict kilns—an unusual and interesting spot for a picnic. Next is a hilly 1½ miles, with views to the steep cove of Porth Llanlleiana

Northern Anglesey

and the flashing light on the Skerries in the distance behind Wylfa. Pass a right turning to Llanbadrig Church. Take the next right fork for Cemaes Bay, signed car park. Cycle down the lane to the car park by the beach. Go through the bollards and along the prom. There are toilets and a kiosk selling drinks, ices and snacks at the beach.

Turn right to cross the bridge over a lovely river into **Cemaes Bay**. Pass the Harbour Hotel and then the Stag (there is another beach down the lane behind this pub) and Ye Old Vigour Inn. Cycle through the town passing shops, a chip shop, the village hall with a clocktower, a garage with a delightful old bicycle advert and the Woburn Hill Hotel.

At the next roundabout go straight across, **with care**, signed Llanfechell into Ffordd y Felin. Pass the attractively converted mill, go uphill then down again and turn first left signed Llanfechell by the huge pylons. This next ¾ mile is in common with the Cemlyn Bay Ride. In the village of **Llanfechell** pass Coed Crafts (open Mon-Fri), the church of St Mechell with a stone tower, then the Chapel Libanus, with dates of 1832 and 1903, and a pub, Y Cefn Glas. (The Cemlyn Bay Ride turns right by the pub.) Go straight on and ¼ mile after the village turn left opposite Bryn Clyni. The next few miles are very rural.

Go up and down then straight on at Tai Hen, signed Amlwch. After a mile along this lane with neat hedges turn left, at the chapel, along a quiet undulating lane. Go down over a stream and up again. At the end turn right, **with care**, at the T-junction onto a wider road. After ½ mile turn first left onto a minor road. In ½ mile, where there is a sharp left bend and a road joining on the right, decide on the shorter Off-Road or the longer Road Route.

OFF-ROAD ROUTE
Turn right and immediately left onto a green track. This crosses the railway by a humpback bridge. It is a very boggy and grassy track for ¼ mile and it may be necessary to walk some of it unless you have mountain bike, but it does provide a challenge! After ¼ mile there is a cross roads by an old chapel. Go straight across to rejoin the Main Route.

ROAD ROUTE
Continue round the left bend, cross a humpback bridge and after ½ mile turn sharp right at the end. In ½ mile, by an old chapel, turn left into a narrow unmarked track.

MAIN ROUTE continued...
This narrow lane was originally asphalted and is easier riding than the green lane but has puddles after wet weather. After ½ mile at the T-junction turn left and pass the school. At the next junction on the outskirts of Amlwch there is a leisure centre and windmill to the left. Turn right here. After ¼ mile at the staggered junction turn right onto the B5111 and immediately left. (An emergency short cut back to Bull Bay is to turn left onto the B5111 and ride back through Amlwch.) Then after ½ mile turn right, **with care**, onto the A5025. Turn first left, signed Llaneilian, after ½ mile. Pass Penmaen Hostel (self catering) and go downhill for a mile. At the T-junction decide whether to do the **Llaneilian detour** or not.

MAIN ROUTE continued...
Turn left signed Porth Amlwch along Llaneilian Road. After a mile, soon reaching the houses and chapels, go downhill to **Porth Amlwch**. It is a busy harbour with both fishing boats and pleasure craft. Pass the Pilot Stores and Harbour fish and chip shop and 2 small pubs, the Adelphi and the Liverpool Arms. There is a derelict windmill on the hill above the port. Then continue straight on in Machine Street/Stryd y Glorian. Turn right, **with care**, onto the main road and cross the level crossing. Turn first left into the old part of the town on Wesley Street passing terraced houses and the Bull Inn. In the centre of **Amlwch** pass St Eleth church with a stone

tower opposite the Dinorben Arms and turn right by a cafe onto Ffordd Llechog/Bull Bay Road. Turn right, **with care**, onto the A5025 to return to the start, after a mile on the main road, passing the church shaped like an upturned boat.

LLANEILIAN DETOUR extra 2 miles each way to lighthouse

Turn right at the T-junction by the bus stop and cycle down to the small bay passing the old church which is well worth a visit. The lane which comes in on the right is the link from Ride 4. Pass a telephone, a small car park and toilets. At the tiny roundabout you can leave the bikes secured and go onto the shingly beach or continue on the surfaced lane for a lovely ride to the castellated lighthouse. There are wonderful views from this promontory as it commands a wide sweep of the sea. There are plenty of wild flowers adapted to the salt laden spray (fifteen still in flower one late November). If you walk round the outside of this automatic lighthouse be careful not to look directly into the light as it is very bright, nor to be deafened by the foghorn in misty weather! Return by the same route, climbing gently back up to the bend at the bus stop, where you continue by rejoining the Main Route.

OTHER INFORMATION

BULL BAY/PORTH LLECHOG
At the start of the 19th century Bull Bay was a busy fishing and shipbuilding port. Now it is a peaceful rocky and shingly cove ideal for cliff walks and an afternoon on the beach browsing round the rock pools.

PORTH WEN is the site of the derelict Cemais brickworks and the beehive shaped kilns and other remains are interesting. It operated from 1850 to 1914. At present there is a debate about the conservation of this area for its industrial archaeology. There is a wonderful limestone arch here showing the power of the sea in creating weird shaped stacks in the rock.

DINAS GYNFOR
This is the largest Celtic hill fort in Anglesey. It is on the cliffs and reached by a short footpath to the west of Hell's Mouth. It is the northernmost point in Wales. It was built by the chieftain Cynfor and may have been the site of the last resistance of the Celts to the conquering Romans. If you visit during a winter gale you will appreciate why Hell's Mouth was so called!

CEMAES BAY/BAE CEMAIS
This was also an important, if tiny harbour, in the last century before Amlwch took over the role. It was even reputed to be the haunt of smugglers but is now a quiet village with a choice of five good beaches, some of shingle and some of sand. Llanbadrig church is the only one on the island dedicated to St Patrick, the patron

saint of Ireland. Local legend has it that he was shipwrecked on Mouse Island and then took refuge in a cave at Cemaes and founded the church on the cliff here in thanks. The holy water from the well was believed to cure most ills. The district tourist association is at 16 High Street.

LLANEILIAN

It is believed that a church was built here in the 5th century by a Cambrian Prince called Caswallon in honour of St Eilian. The present church dates from the 12th to 15th centuries. The spire has an unusual shape being like a pyramid. The key may be obtained from 'Pedwar Gwynt'. Inside the church is a sinister skeleton on the rood screen saying 'Colyn angau yw pechod' meaning 'Sin is the sting of death'! The chancel roof has engravings of seaweed and the corbels have angels playing trumpets and bagpipes! The church used to have a pair of Dog Tongs with which the church warden used to eject quarrelling dogs during the services! An old wooden chest has a legend that if you could climb inside it on the first of January you would survive the next year. There are several graves of schooner captains in the churchyard. The portrait of St Eilian shows him with 5 fingers and a thumb instead of the more usual 4! The Porth is a beauty spot, the cove beach is mainly pebbly but has a dramatic setting with high cliffs. On the headland of Point Lynas is a modern lighthouse guiding shipping through the dangerous waters. The pilot station was started in 1766 when Liverpool became an important port. There are prominent radio masts on the hill of Mynedd Eilian.

AMLWCH

Amlwch means 'near the loch', referring to a lake which was found between the port and church. Nearby Parys Mountain has been mined for copper since Roman times. Amlwch had the largest population on Anglesey in the early 19th century. In its heyday 1500 men, women and children worked at the mine and produced more copper annually than Cornwall. In the 18th century Britain's copper currency was in a poor state and in short supply and more small change was needed for everyday dealings so the Parys Mine Company of Amlwch were the first to mint provincial tokens called the Anglesey Penny. Some can be seen in Oriel Ynys Mon. They had an excellent design with a Druid's head on one side and were dated between 1787 and 1793. The mine closed near the end of the 19th century because of changing copper prices and competition from America and Africa. The place today is a sad reminder of the environmental ravages caused by uncontrolled opencast mining. It is also very dangerous having deep shafts. Some of the streams are very acidic. It is interesting in that some of the grasses have evolved tolerance to the poisonous copper in the soil and thrive on the old slag heaps.

At **Porth Amlwch** you can see the harbour which was built in 1793 for the export of copper by sea. Some of the ore was smelted in kilns here. The remains of the shipbuilding sheds can also be seen. Amlwch regained importance between 1973 and

1987 when Shell's Marine Oil Terminal operated here. Half million tonne tankers used to offload oil from the North Sea and Arabian Gulf to the pipeline which took it to Stanlow for refining. The terminal is on the far side of the hillock behind the port and still exudes rather unpleasant fuel smells.

THE PUBS

The Trecastell Hotel (Robinsons) and the Bull Bay Hotel both do bar meals and welcome children. Both are at Bull Bay.

The Harbour Hotel (free house) (children welcome) and the Stag (Burtonwood) both do bar meals and are in Cemaes Bay.

Ye Old Vigour is also in Cemaes Bay as is the Woburn Hill Hotel (free house) which has a restaurant and does bar meals.

There are cafes in Cemaes Bay and Amlwch.

RIDE 6

CEMLYN TO
CHURCH BAY (PORTH SWTAN)

ROUTE	Cemlyn—Tregele—Llanfechell—Llanfflewyn—Llanrhyddlad—Rhydwyn—Church Bay/Porth Swtan—Llanfairynghornwy—Cemlyn
DISTANCE	15 miles/24 km. Cemlyn Loop 8 miles, Llanrhyddlad to Church Bay Loop 9 miles.
ASCENT	230 metres. Hilly.
START	Cemlyn, Grid Ref 337932 (or Mynachdy or Llanrhyddlad)
TO START	About 1½ miles from the A5025 between Valley and Amlwch

Allow 3 hours at a leisurely pace. This is the most hilly route we do on Anglesey but is exhilarating and well worth the effort. Check brakes (not to mention youngsters' braking skills!) before the hills. The ride has brilliant views of the sea, the Skerries and the lighthouse. There are car parks at Cemlyn and Mynachdy. Coming from Menai Bridge we prefer to start at Llanrhyddlad, but there is only roadside parking.

It is best to use it as 2 separate short rides with young children by using the lane across the middle of this route from the church in Llanfairynghornwy to Llanfechell passing near Llyn Llygeirian.

You will have many opportunities for diversions on foot as there are many footpaths in the area but no bridleways. There are plenty of good picnic spots. It is excellent for ornithologists at Cemlyn but essential to keep away from the shingle when the birds are nesting, mainly in May and June.

There are links with the Church Bay to Llynon Mill Ride in Llanrhyddlad. We do the route clockwise as there are no particularly dangerous right turns.

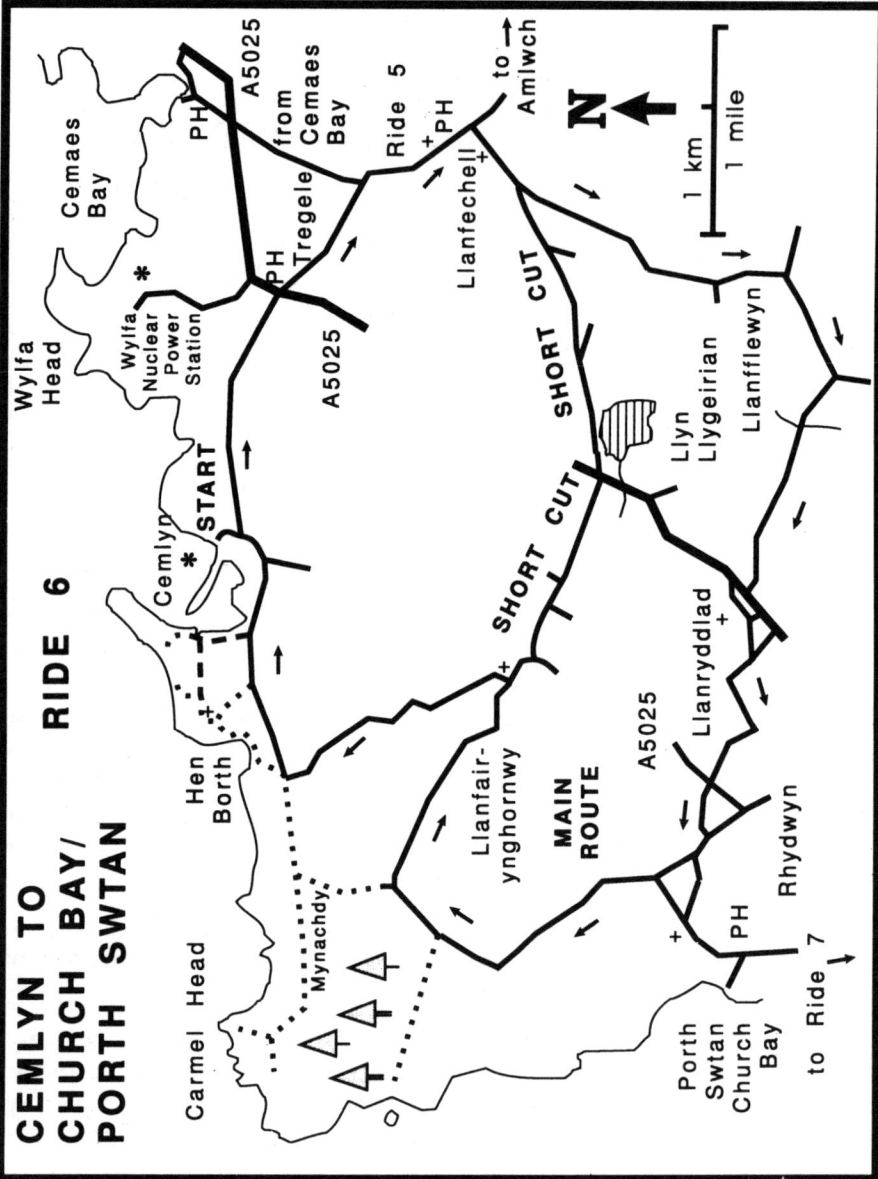

CEMLYN TO CHURCH BAY / PORTH SWTAN

RIDE 6

Cemaes Bay

A5025

from Cemaes Bay

Ride 5

to Amlwch

N

1 km
1 mile

PH

Tregele

PH

Wylfa Nuclear Power Station

Llanfechell +PH

SHORT CUT

Wylfa Head

A5025

Llyn Llygeirian

Llanfflewyn

Cemlyn

START

SHORT CUT

Llanrhyddlad

A5025

Hen Borth

Llanfair-ynghornwy

MAIN ROUTE

PH

Rhydwyn

Carmel Head

Mynachdy

Porth Swtan Church Bay

to Ride 7

THE RIDE

MAIN ROUTE 15 miles

From the car park at **Cemlyn** cycle to the road and turn left. It is then 1½ miles to the main road. At the A5025 is the Douglas Arms and a store in the small village of **Tregele**. Turn right, **with care**, and immediately left, passing a free range pig farm, where you may be lucky in seeing lots of piglets lined up by their mums for the milk bar!

Some of us take our exercise by bicycle!

(**Or** for a diversion to visit **Wylfa** Nuclear Power Station, turn left onto the A5025 and first left, and return by the same route.)

After ½ mile turn right signed Llanfechell by some pylons. Pass Coed Crafts (selling decorative wall butterflies) and a caravan site just before the next village. In **Llanfechell** is the church of St Mechell with a tower sporting a fish weather vane on a hexagonal squat stone spire. Pass the war memorial, clock, post office and shop. Turn right by the pub, Y Cefn Glas, and continue to the end of the ribbon style settlement passing the school and chapel. Then decide on the Short Cut or Main Route. To continue on the main route turn left at the fork.

SHORT CUT (*or 2 separate short rides: **Cemlyn Loop**, 8 miles; using these lanes in the opposite direction for **Llanrhyddlad to Church Bay Loop**, 9 miles*)
Turn right at the fork, opposite the sign for Llanfechell. It is 1½ miles to the A5025, passing Llyn Llygeirian on the left. Go straight across the main road, **with care**, signed Llanfairynghornwy. After just over a mile you reach a T-junction. Turn right and pass the church in Llanfairynghornwy. Turn right to rejoin the Main Route on the way to Cemlyn.

MAIN ROUTE continued...
It is ½ mile climb up to Mynedd Mechell, passing a converted windmill. After ¾ mile pass a post office. Carry on for a mile uphill through the scattered hamlet of Llanfflewyn. At the summit turn sharp right and cycle downhill, passing sheep fields. Go under pylons and straight on for a mile to the main road, the A5025. Turn right, **with care**, and immediately first left to **Llanrhyddlad**. Its church and row of houses stand out with a prominent facade. (There is some parking space at the right hand end of the village on a bit of the old road which is now a dead end.)

In Llanrhyddlad pass the church and telephone and go straight on (not left back to the main road). Turn right at the T-junction and then follow the sign for Porth Swtan (Church Bay). Go straight on at the cross roads and then at the T-junction turn right by the village sign for **Rhydwyn**.

After ¼ mile take the right fork up a very narrow, steep lane or left for a diversion down to **Church Bay**. It is worth the detour if you haven't visited it on Ride 7, despite the extra climbing on the return!

Climb up the hill which gives good views to Holyhead (pass the lane joining on the left which is the short but steep way up the hill from the Church Bay detour).

There is a gorsey heath on the left (Pen y Foel) and low walls covered with earth. They are splendid with gold celandine flowers in spring and rich purple knapweed in summer. Go straight on (not right to the trig point at the top of Mynedd y Garn) and follow the winding lane down the hill.

Pass an unfenced farm with hens, cockerels, guard dogs and geese. On one occasion a fast speed past these was found to be useful and promoted even faster speeds when the geese gave chase! There are stupendous views to the Skerries and the lighthouse. There is a dark green conifer plantation ahead, unusual in this part of the island and making a pleasant contrast with the rest of the landscape.

Continue right round the bend and after a mile reach **Llanfairynghornwy**. Pass the post office, which sells sweets, and has a notice warning Mormons and Jehovah's Witnesses to keep away! Turn next left signed Cemlyn. The next mile is mainly downhill with views over a pleasant valley with some trees. At the bottom of the hill fork right (not straight on to Cerau).

St Rhyddlad's church at Church Bay

There is a sharp right bend by a small **car park** (Mynachdy) for Tyn Llan and Hen Borth. After ½ mile there is another shorter footpath to Tyn Llan. After ½ mile you will reach the large lagoon at **Cemlyn**. Turn left into the car park and Trwyn Cemlyn or continue past the lagoon and turn left and next left again to the main car park by the shingle spit (NB not open in May and June).

OTHER INFORMATION

CEMLYN

The name Cemlyn comes from Cam—bent and Llyn—lake. The whole area is owned by the NT. The huge brick wall was constructed by Captain Vivien Hewitt from Bryn Aber who used to manage the lagoon as a sanctuary for the birds. The lagoon is the winter refuge for mallard, teal, widgeon, little grebe, tufted duck, goldeneye, shoveller and coot. It is a North Wales Wildlife Trust Nature Reserve, mainly famous for its tern colony in summer, but gulls, mallard, shelduck, swans, red breasted merganser, coot and moorhens also breed here. Since some birds nest on the shingle you need to be very careful if you walk along the ridge and you are asked not to walk on the crest or lagoon side between May and the middle of August.

The plants are interesting too. Sea kale, sea pink, sea campion, sea aster, sea purslane and sea beet are names which leave you in no doubt about the plants' maritime preferences! For further information contact NWWT, 376 High St, Bangor, Gwynedd LL57 1YE, tel 01248 351545.

The area abounds in legends from the past. Cemlyn was reputedly the haunt of pirates. Llanrhydrys church, west of Cemlyn, was thought to have been founded in AD 570 and the present building dates from the 12th and 13th centuries. Further west, Mynachdy, meaning Monks' House, is on the site of a very old monastic building and there is supposedly a passage from the cellars to a seaside cave where the monks hid their treasures!

WYLFA NUCLEAR POWER STATION
The observation tower is open to public and there are guided tours. There is a short Nature Trail in the grounds. Its vital statistics are fairly staggering, it has a capacity of 1 million kilowatts and uses seawater for cooling at a rate of 55 billion gallons per hour. The rumours that the grass glows in the dark round here are unsubstantiated!

PORTH SWTAN See Ride 7.

LLANFAIRYNGHORNWY
Two important innovations come from the area. One was the founding of the 'Anglesey Association for the Preservation of Life from Shipwreck' by Frances Williams, who with his wife raised funds for lifeboats for Anglesey and set up the first lifeboat station on the North Wales coast. Its second source of fame was for its 'bonesetters', one of whom perfected the splint—an important invention as anyone who has had a broken bone will appreciate!

CARMEL HEAD
This is a wonderful place to visit on foot. It has forest, heath and cliff habitats and is good for wildlife.

THE SKERRIES
This is a Viking name, the Welsh name is Ynysoedd y Moelrhoniaid or the Island of the Seals. The lighthouse dates from 1714.

LLANFECHELL
This village is a conservation area due to its square. It was the site of a hiring fair, at which farmers hired their farm labourers. The church has a 16th century tower on the top of which is a rather crude stumpy spire. Apparently this was added in the 18th century by the local squire who thought that the loud tolling of the bells was souring his beer and ordered the spire to muffle the sound!

THE PUBS
The Douglas Arms in Tregele (Free House) serves bar meals and children are welcome.
Y Cefn Glas in Llanfechell (Bass) serves bar meals.

RIDE 7

LLANFACHRAETH TO LLYNON MILL
AND CHURCH BAY

ROUTE	Llanfachraeth—Llanddeusant—Llynon Mill— Llanrhyddlad—Church Bay/Porth Swtan—Porth Trefadog—Porth Trywyn Mawr—Llanfwrog— Llanfachraeth.
DISTANCE	13 miles/21 km
ASCENT	120 metres. Undulating.
START	Llanfachraeth, Grid Ref 316821.
TO START	A5025, 2½ miles north of Valley. There is a layby just before the village on the right by the first house.

A windmill and beaches off the beaten track (literally and littorally!) are some of the delights on this route. There are excellent views. The lanes are quiet and there is a choice of some off-road cycling. The tracks beside the sea are actually roads, but are not maintained. Their surfaces vary and include stones, grass and sand. Mountain bikers will really enjoy them. A couple of crossings of an A road need care but it is usually fairly quiet. One very short steep hill downwards requires good brakes. As well as the pubs, the cafe at Church Bay and at the mill serve refreshments.

The start is at the tiny village of Llanfachraeth for several reasons; it is the nearest point on the ride to Holyhead and the more populated part of Anglesey, there is a layby for parking and it keeps cars off the route! This ride links with Ride 8 at a couple of places and with Ride 6 between Llanrhyddlad and Church Bay.

THE RIDE

MAIN ROUTE 13 miles

Cycle into **Llanfachraeth** and pass the river and cemetery on the A5025. Turn right at the post office opposite the Holland Arms. Go straight on for a mile. Turn left at a T-junction following signs for Llynon Mill by the Chapel Ty'n y Maen 1904. In about 1 mile at the next crossroads on the outskirts of Llanddeusant turn left and reach **Llynon Mill** after ½ mile. This

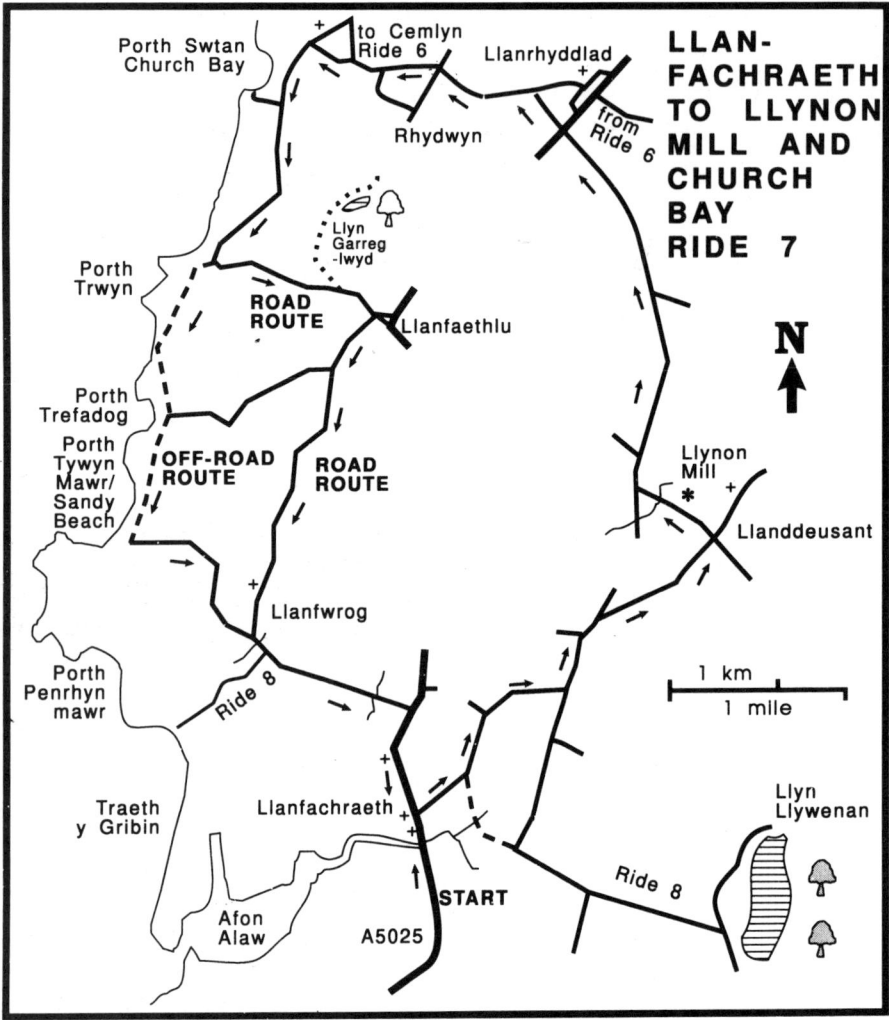

LLAN-
FACHRAETH
TO LLYNON
MILL AND
CHURCH
BAY
RIDE 7

Porth Swtan
Church Bay

to Cemlyn
Ride 6

Llanrhyddlad

from Ride 6

Rhydwyn

Llyn
Garreg
-lwyd

Porth
Trwyn

ROAD
ROUTE

Llanfaethlu

N

Porth
Trefadog

Llynon
Mill

Porth
Tywyn
Mawr/
Sandy
Beach

OFF-ROAD
ROUTE

ROAD
ROUTE

Llanddeusant

Llanfwrog

Porth
Penrhyn
mawr

Ride 8

1 km

1 mile

Traeth
y Gribin

Llanfachraeth

Llyn
Llywenan

START

Ride 8

Afon
Alaw

A5025

point interlinks with Ride 8.

Turn right back onto the lane after visiting the mill and in ½ mile at the T-junction turn right by a post box. Continue straight on, through farmland with a variety of animals, following signs for Llanrhyddlad and Cemaes. After an undulating couple of miles you will reach the A5025. Turn right, **with care**, and immediately left and pass the Island Pottery (Crochendy Ynys) in **Llanrhyddlad**. You could link with Ride 6 here.

Follow signs for Church Bay (Porth Swtan) by bending left. This lane has a profusion of wild flowers in the bank with lady's smock, bluebells, celandine, hedge parsley, English comfrey, herb robert and violets. Go straight on at the cross

Llynon Mill

roads. There are good views of the gorse clad hill and over the bay to Holyhead and plenty more flowers on the verges such as foxglove, pennywort, campion and scabious.

At the T-junction, by the sign for the edge of Rhydwyn, turn right. Pass the Church Bay Inn and the church of St Rhyddlad with its impressive spire. It is then very steeply down hill and round a sharp bend where **care** is needed. After climbing a small hill turn right signed **Church Bay** and pass the Lobster Pot cafe, toilets, car park, and Wave Crest cafe: time for a rest and refreshments or a chance to visit the beach! Return uphill to the T-junction and turn right. This lovely lane runs parallel to the coast for a mile to Borth Wen at Porth Trywyn. Decide here whether to do the Off-Road or the Road Route.

ROAD ROUTE 3 miles
Continue on the lane for a mile to the outskirts of **Llanfaethlu**. Turn first right signed Llanfwrog. Pass a telephone, go down a hill and up again to Llanfwrog. There are good views of the sea and Holy Island.

OFF-ROAD ROUTE 3 miles
There is an old farm on the left with tiny barns and a very sharp bend to

the left where you leave the road and turn right onto a track which is surfaced initially. Cross a stream by the beach and go through a gate onto a muddy track which closely follows the bottom of the field, following the overhead wires at first. (Secure all gates and do not stray from the track.) It becomes surfaced rather better again at Porth Trefadog.

Cross the beach at Porth Trefadog, then ascend by the grassy track and descend where it becomes sandy. It should be no hardship to walk above or across this pleasant beach. It isn't far to the road where you can cycle again. After a mile pass a right turning for Sandy Bay. It is then ½ mile to Llanfwrog. At the T-junction turn right. The Road Route rejoins here.

MAIN ROUTE continued...
In Llanfwrog pass a telephone and attractive cottages. Keep left and pass a chapel. It is a mile to the A5025 (in common with Ride 8). Turn right, **with care**, to return along the main road for only ¾ mile back to Llanfachraeth, passing another chapel, church and school.

OTHER INFORMATION

LLYNON MILL
See Ride 8. The mill is open 11.30-3.30 but closed on Mondays and open less often in winter. There is a small admission charge.

CHURCH BAY/PORTH SWTAN
Swtan means either Cove of the Swedes as legend has it that Vikings landed here, or Cove of the Whiting according to another source! It has a quiet, mainly pebbly beach with good cliff walks. The English name is from the church overlooking the bay.

LLANFACHRAETH
It is a small village with several good beaches nearby. Porth Trefadog is the site of an ancient hill fort. Porth Trywyn Mawr is good for bathing and Porth Penrhyn Mawr is shingly. Traeth y Gribin has dangerous currents. Llanfwrog churchyard has a gravestone with a poem commemorating two unknown sailors.

THE PUBS
Holland Hotel (Lees Real Ale) is in Llanfachraeth.
Church Bay Inn (Tetleys, Wrexham Lager) is at Church Bay has a terrace and serves bar and restaurant meals.

RIDE 8

BODEDERN TO LLYN LLYWENAN
AND LLYNON MILL

ROUTE	Bodedern—Presaddfed Burial Chamber—Llyn Llywenan—Howell Water Mill—Elim—Llanddeusant—Llynon Mill—detour to beach and link to Ride 7—Afon Alaw—Bodedern
DISTANCE	12 miles/19 km + Extra Loop 4 miles + beach detour 4 miles. Total 20 miles.
ASCENT	120 metres. Undulating.
START	Bodedern, Grid Ref 333800
TO START	From the A5 between Llangefni and Holyhead, turn right opposite the road to RAF Valley onto the minor road for 1 mile to Bodedern. Park in the layby on the right opposite the school.

It may look a strange shaped route on the map but there is much of interest here. We see Anglesey's only water wheel and working windmill as well as an ancient burial chamber, a pretty lake and a remote beach. It is an expedition which recaptures images of the past.

Although undulating, the Main Route is a short ride and the lanes are very rural. To make a longer route there is an Extra Loop on very quiet lanes as well as the beach detour. There is a ½ mile off-road alternative and the ½ mile past Howell Mill is also on a track unsuitable for vehicles. The ride takes about 2 hours at a leisurely pace. Binoculars would be useful for bird watching at the lake and beach. Refreshments can be found at the mill or there are many excellent picnic places.

It can link with Ride 9 at Llantrisant or Ride 7 at the Mill for those wanting a longer route. There is also a short section in common with Ride 7 on the Detour from Llanfachraeth to the beach.

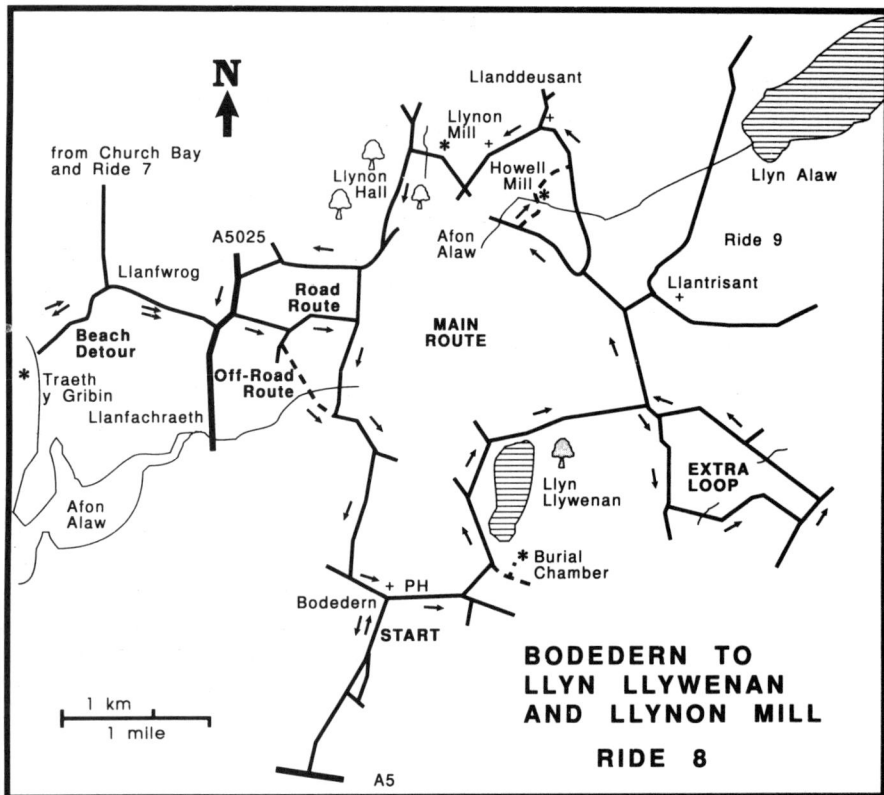

N

from Church Bay
and Ride 7

Llanddeusant

Llynon
Mill

Howell
Mill

Llyn Alaw

Llynon
Hall

A5025

Afon
Alaw

Ride 9

Llanfwrog

Road
Route

Llantrisant

Beach
Detour

MAIN
ROUTE

Traeth
y Gribin

Off-Road
Route

Llanfachraeth

Llyn
Llywenan

EXTRA
LOOP

Afon
Alaw

Burial
Chamber

+ PH

Bodedern

START

1 km

1 mile

**BODEDERN TO
LLYN LLYWENAN
AND LLYNON MILL**

RIDE 8

A5

THE RIDE

MAIN ROUTE 12 miles

From the layby opposite the school, Ysgol Uwchradd Bodedern and the Canolfan Bro Alaw, turn right and cycle through the village of Bodedern on London Road. Pass the workshops, Gilgal chapel, shops, one selling ice creams, the George pub, and a telephone. At the T-junction turn right into Church Road, the B5109, and pass the church and Y Goron pub. ½ mile beyond the village turn left onto a lane. In less than ½ mile on the bend turn right to Presaddfed Burial Chamber, signed Anglesey Shooting. It is about ¼ mile along the track. Leave the bikes by the gate to visit this interesting site. Return to the lane and turn right.

There are pleasant views over the lake. After ½ mile fork right then in ¼ mile fork right again. There is a good picnic spot by the lake with plenty of birds to watch through the reeds. It is good for lakeside flowers as well such as sneezewort, silverweed, willowherbs and meadowsweet. The first house on the left after the lake is delightfully named 'Pooh Corner'! The Ainon chapel at Pen-llyn dates from 1881. There are old walls and banks down the lane covered with earth and a profusion of wild flowers such as scabious, honeysuckle, St John's wort and hedge parsley. It seems reminiscent of Cornwall. A mile from the lake decide whether to include the Extra Loop. To omit this just continue straight on at this junction, signed Llanddeusant, Llanfaethlu and Llynon Mill.

EXTRA LOOP 4 miles

Turn first right, signed Trefor and A5. Go straight on in a few yards, where the lane from our return joins on the left and pass a weather station. It is a pleasant lane for ¾ mile with scattered trees. Turn first left signed Clwch Nursery. (There is an application for planning permission here to build a wind farm with 36 turbines—another sustainable energy supply—we see them all on this ride!) The lane is quite narrow with a grassy middle. It goes downhill, crosses a tiny stream and then becomes unsurfaced and climbs gently uphill. Turn left onto the B5112 opposite a house and chapel (Llachcynfarwy). After ¼ mile turn first left, signed the herb nursery. Pass Cae Gwyn, cross the tiny stream and continue along this narrow lane for a mile. It is also somewhat grassy in the middle. At the end turn right and retrace the outward route for a few yards. Turn right at the end to rejoin the Main Route.

MAIN ROUTE continued...

After ¾ mile go straight on. (The lane to the right provides a link with Ride 9.) In ¼ mile turn left signed Mill and Llanfaethlu. After ½ mile turn first right by the post box, by a small sign for Howell Mill. It is a very narrow single track lane. After only a few yards you reach the mill. There are often argumentative ducks and geese here. Follow the left bend down the hill and round the mill. The huge water wheel is behind the building.

Cross the stream. It is a delightful wooded valley. Climb up for ¼ mile and pass the Elim campsite. At the T-junction turn left by the Horeb Baptist chapel then, after ½ mile at the edge of Llanddeusant, turn left by the Bethania chapel. Go down past the telephone and church with a stone spire. There is a converted church on the opposite side. Pass the post office, village pump and another old chapel. Then turn right at the cross road, signed the Mill. It is only ¼ mile to Llynon Mill.

After a visit to the mill turn right back onto the lane to continue the ride. Go downhill to the T-junction and turn left. It is a very beautiful stream valley with bluebells in spring. Unfortunately Dutch Elm Disease has taken its toll of the lovely old elms and most have been felled. Pass Llynon Hall surrounded by beautiful mature trees, unusual for Anglesey. There are also strips of relict woodland along the lane. Turn right at the T-junction then first right along a narrow lane. Climb up a short hill, to a height of 44 metres, with a view to Holyhead. It is a good glide down for ½ mile to a stream valley (but beware of a bend at the bottom). We now join a bit of the original A road. The old bridge is visible on the right. Turn left onto the A5025 and follow it for only ¼ mile. Decide whether to do the beach detour or not. If omitting the detour, turn left onto a narrow lane.

DETOUR TO BEACH 4 miles
Turn right, **with care**, signed Tywyn Mawr/Sandy Beach, Llanfwrog and, Penrhyn. The next mile is in common with Ride 7 but we visit a different beach. After a mile keep left at the grassy triangle. It is ¾ mile down to the beach along a narrow but surfaced lane.

We reach the top end of Traeth y Gribin beach. It is a very quiet spot—ideal for a picnic or leaving the bikes for a stroll. Across the strait is Holy Island and the skyline is dominated by the Anglesey Aluminium chimney. The sand and mud flats are good for wading birds.

Retrace your route back up the lane, bearing right onto the lane at Llanfwrog. At the top turn left onto the main road, the A5025. Turn immediately right, **with care**, onto a narrow lane.

MAIN ROUTE continued...
At the end of the lane decide on the Off-Road Route or Main Route.

OFF-ROAD ROUTE
Turn right and immediately first left into a green lane. It can be very

overgrown in summer and is one only for the off-road enthusiast. It is downhill and manageable if you have a mountain bike.

Off-road in winter

It is ½ mile down to a stream, the Afon Alaw. Cross it by a footbridge and continue. The lane becomes surfaced where another track joins from the right. At the next T-junction turn right and rejoin the Main Route at *.

MAIN ROUTE continued ...
Turn left and continue for ½ mile. Turn right at the T-junction and follow the lane for ½ mile, passing a chapel at Llanfigael. Cross a stream and go round a sharp left bend where the Off-Road Route rejoins from the right *.

Go under the pylons and keep straight on. There is a standing stone in the field on the right. After a mile at the T-junction turn left onto the B5109, signed Bodedern. In the village turn right, **with care**, into London Road/Ffordd Lundain. Retrace the outward route back to the car park opposite the school.

OTHER INFORMATION
LLYNON MILL/MELIN LLYNON
It is the only working windmill in Wales. It was originally built between 1775-6 but had lain derelict for many years before being restored. For its period it shows an amazing amount of automation, the huge canvas sails catch the wind and turn

three giant millstones as well as providing the power to raise hoists to lift the grain. The mill is open on Tuesday to Saturday from 11-5 and on Sundays from 1-5. It is open less often in winter. Small entrance charge, tel 01407 840845.

THE HOWELL MILL/MELIN HYWEL

Howell Mill

This is privately owned. It has been in use for 600 years! After restoration in 1975, it won a conservation award in 1978 from the RICS (Royal Institute of Chartered Surveyors). It has an overshot water wheel which still works and mainly grinds cereal for animal feed. It may be possible to visit in summer.

LLYN LLEWENAN
This is Anglesey's largest natural lake and has deciduous woods beyond.

PRESADDFED
This is a Neolithic burial chamber covered originally by a mound of earth or stones dating from 4000-2000 BC. It was used for communal burial of the dead.

BODEDERN
Bodedern means the house at St Edern. It is on the original Holyhead to London

route hence the road name London Road. Eventually the A5 route was altered to bypass Llangefni, and Bodedern became a more isolated village. It is near to RAF Valley. Farm Life/Fferm Fyw, Bodowyr, Bodedern is half way between the A5 and Bodedern. It is a working farm open to the public between 10 and dusk. It has the usual animals and displays, coffee bar and shop. Small admission charge, tel 01407 741171.

AFON ALAW
Bedd Branwen is a Bronze Age burial mound built round an earlier standing stone and is the legendary site of Branwen's grave. Welsh folk lore tells of how the beautiful Branwen died of a broken heart. It is marked by a boulder on the banks of the river just south west of Llanddeusant (Grid Ref 361859). 5th century amber beads from the Baltic and jet beads from Yorkshire have been found here. There is also a standing stone at Grid Ref 342832 called Tregwehelydd.

Llanfachraeth See Ride 7.

THE PUBS
The Crown Inn/Y Goron (Burtonwood) is in Bodedern and serves hot and cold bar food and has accommodation.

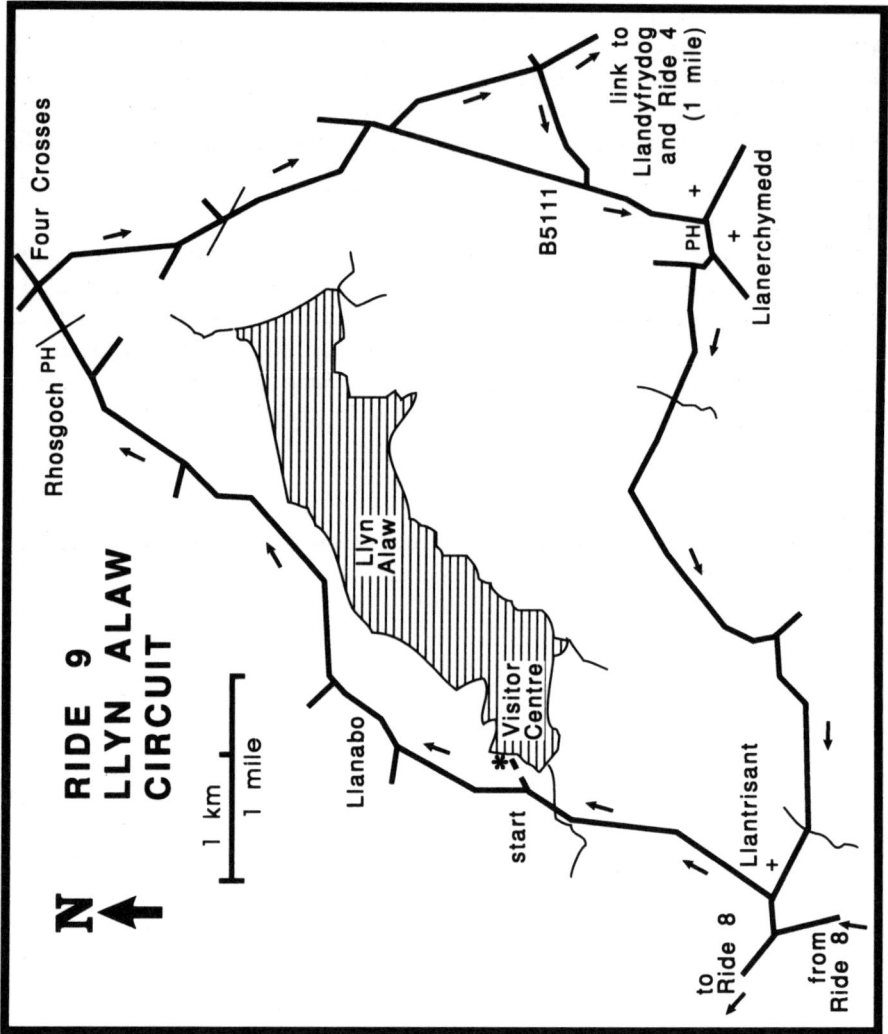

RIDE 9
LLYN ALAW
CIRCUIT

N

1 km
1 mile

Four Crosses

Rhosgoch PH

Llanabo

Llyn Alaw

Visitor Centre

start

B5111

link to
Llandyfrydog
and Ride 4
(1 mile)

PH

Llanerchymedd

Llantrisant

to Ride 8

from Ride 8

RIDE 9

LLYN ALAW CIRCUIT

ROUTE	Llyn Alaw Visitor Centre—Llanabo—Rhosgoch—Llanerchymedd—Llantrisant—Llyn Alaw Visitor Centre
DISTANCE	14 miles/22 km
ASCENT	200 metres. Undulating.
START	Llyn Alaw Visitor Centre car park (50p pay and display), Grid Ref 373855.
TO START	Take the A5 north-west from Llangefni and turn right onto the B5112 for 2 miles to Trefor. Turn left onto the B5109 and first right in ¼ mile onto a minor road for 2 miles. Turn right and in 200 yards first left in Llantrisant (beware of cyclists). In a mile turn right signed Llyn Alaw and park by the Visitor Centre.

Although it is rather undulating the route is fairly short and the lanes are very quiet; the usual vehicles encountered being tractors. It takes 2½-3 hours at a leisurely pace. The route is described clockwise for a change as there are no dangerous right turns but beware of one roundabout in Llanerchymedd. The navigation is easy as there are only a few junctions. It is a good route for bird watchers and worth taking binoculars at least to the start. Refreshments can be found in Rhosgoch or Llanerchymedd. The latter is a rather grey town but at least it provides amenities. As usual the hedgerows are best for wild flowers in spring and early summer.

THE RIDE

MAIN ROUTE 14 miles

From the Visitor Centre car park cycle to the minor road and turn right. Go north for a mile with good views over the reservoir to the right. Go straight on signed Rhosgoch where a road joins from the left. Ride through the tiny hamlet of **Llanabo** and follow the main road for 2 miles to the outskirts of Rhosgoch. The Siop Fach Pengarnedd and opposite the Sportsman's Lodge were both open in 1992 but closed in 1994.

(For a short cut to omit Rhosgoch: after ½ mile turn right just before the pylons at the boundary of Rhosgoch by a bungalow and road narrows sign.)

Go straight into **Rhosgoch** and pass the Ring Rhosgoch Hotel beside the railway line. After ¼ mile turn first right at the bus stop (at Four Crosses) signed Llanerchymedd. After ¾ mile turn left and after ¼ mile continue straight on. It is a mile to the B5511. Turn right and immediately left. After ½ mile turn right at the crossroads by a post box. (A standing stone is just visible in the second sheep field on the right opposite a track on the left.)

After ¾ mile at a T-junction turn left onto the B5511 and soon enter **Llanerchymedd**. Pass a playground, war memorial, Bryn Golau Eating House, a garage selling ices and the Twrcyhelyn Arms. Turn right, **with care**, at the roundabout signed Holyhead. (There are a chip shop and toilets to the left.) Pass the post office, telephone, church with a square stone tower and village shop selling ices. Go up the hill and over the railway. Turn immediately right, **with care**, by the house Ty Mawr. Then, opposite the last house in the village turn left (straight on to Llyn Alaw is a dead end).

Back seat driver?

This lane is good for wild flowers with sneezewort, yarrow, hardheads, tormentil, meadowsweet, ragwort, bird's foot trefoil, foxglove, campion, purple vetch, silverweed, selfheal and gorse of course! There is a mixture of black cattle, sheep and horses in the fields. There is an old farm on the corner, with a footpath on the right, sometimes with honking geese and a barking Alsatian. You can begin to see glimpses of Llyn Alaw again.

At the top of the hillock by Chwaen Coch (with amusing rabbits on the gateposts) there are good views of Holyhead mountain and often skeins of geese flying over Llyn Alaw below. There are more flowers now including pennywort, white clover and herb robert. After 2 miles from Llanerchymedd, at the T-junction turn right and cycle downhill for a mile to cross the stream in the bog called Cors y Bol. By the church of St Trisant in **Llantrisant** turn right signed Llyn Alaw for a pleasant but undulating mile back to the lake (or turn left to link with Ride 8). Turn right to return to the lakeside car park and the Visitor Centre.

OTHER INFORMATION

LLYN ALAW

Alaw (Water Lily) is an old name found in the Mabinogion (Welsh legends). This is Anglesey's largest lake and supports a healthy wildfowl population. The bird list includes: common sandpiper, lapwing, grasshopper warbler, dunlin, quail, knot, snow bunting, willow warbler, oystercatcher, ringed plover, peregrine falcon, Bewick swan, hen harrier, widgeon, curlew, white fronted goose, goldeneye, teal, and redwing. But not all can be seen at once, some are winter and some are summer visitors!

The lake is stocked annually with over 15,000 brown trout and rainbow trout. You can hire rowing boats and fishing boats and a special boat for the disabled. The dam was built in 1965-6 and it started filling from then; before that it was a marsh. There is a water treatment works beyond the dam. If you take the short footpath beside the lake you should see lots of flowers, birds and butterflies. The Visitor Centre is open from March to October, houses a small display of some of the wildlife and is manned by a Welsh Water Ranger (tel 01407 730762). There are toilets and picnic tables.

LLANABO

The church is medieval and has a 14th century carving of Saint Pabo, believed to be a British chief who found refuge here. It is beside a stream.

LLANERCHYMEDD

This village once had one of the largest markets in Wales and was famous in the last century for clock and clog making.

THE PUBS

The Ring Rhosgoch Hotel (free house) beer garden, serves food from 12-1.30 and 7-8 and is popular with cyclists.
Bryn Golau Eating House in Llanerchymedd (Marstons) serves bar and restaurant meals and children are welcome.
Twrcyhelyn Arms is also in Llanerchymedd (Lees) and serves bar meals, snacks, tea and coffee.

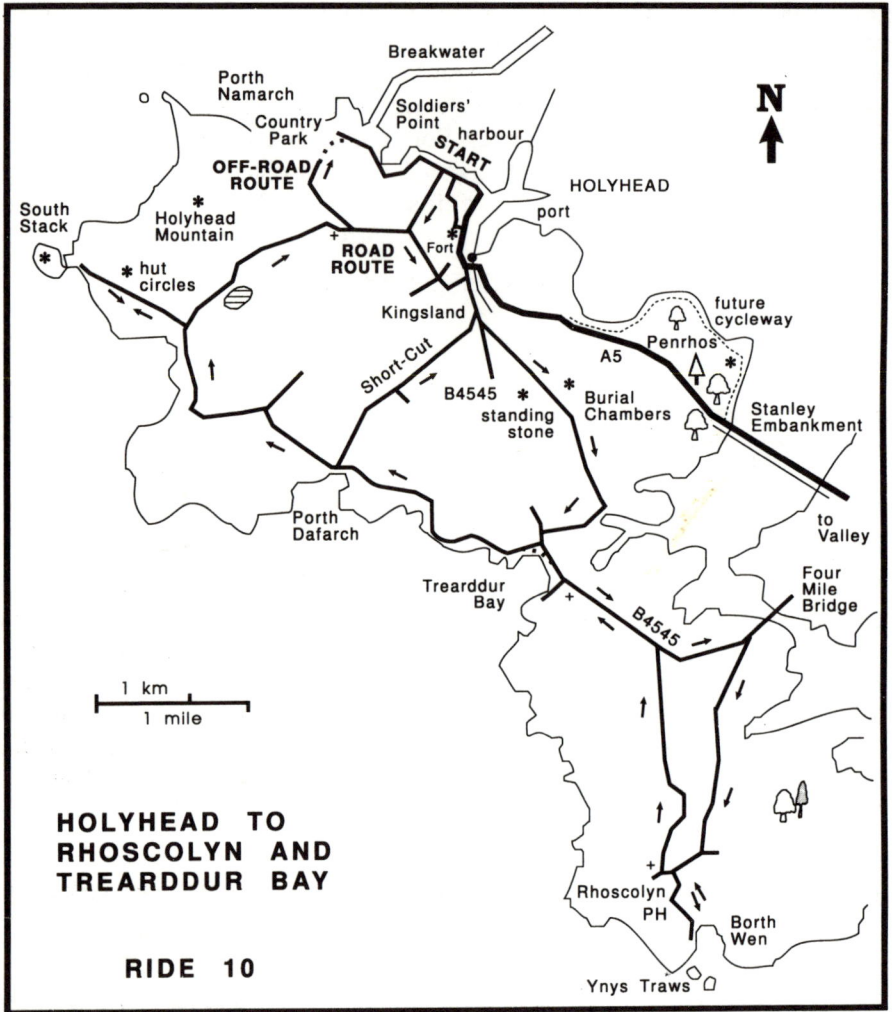

N

Breakwater

Porth
Namarch

o

Country
Park

Soldiers'
Point

harbour

START

HOLYHEAD

**OFF-ROAD
ROUTE**

port

South
Stack

*

Holyhead
Mountain

Fort

* hut
circles

**ROAD
ROUTE**

Kingsland

future
cycleway

Penrhos

A5

*

Short-Cut

B4545 *

standing
stone

*

Burial
Chambers

Stanley
Embankment

Porth
Dafarch

to Valley

Trearddur
Bay

+

B4545

Four
Mile
Bridge

1 km

1 mile

+

Rhoscolyn
PH

Borth
Wen

**HOLYHEAD TO
RHOSCOLYN AND
TREARDDUR BAY**

Ynys Traws

RIDE 10

RIDE 10

HOLYHEAD TO RHOSCOLYN
AND TREARDDUR BAY

ROUTE	Holyhead—Kingsland—Trearddur Bay—(Extra Loop: Four Mile Bridge—Rhoscolyn—Trearddur Bay)—Porth Dafarch—(South Stack detour)—Breakwater Country Park—Holyhead
DISTANCE	17 miles/27 km. Trearddur Bay Loop 10 miles, Rhoscolyn Loop 7½ miles, South Stack detour 2 miles.
ASCENT	140 metres.
START	Holyhead promenade, Grid Ref 244833. Roadside parking or in car park by marina further along prom. OR Trearddur Bay car park.
TO START	BY ROAD Follow A5 from London to the end then turn left! BY FERRY from Dublin

This is a route with several choices. Although about 17 miles in total it can be done as 2 rides: one to Trearddur Bay and one to Rhoscolyn. Holy Island is very narrow in the middle and there is only the one road here, the B4545, so there is an unavoidable, but fairly quiet, mile each way on it to and from Rhoscolyn. There is a Short Cut on a pleasant minor road back from Porth Dafarch to the Kingsland area of Holyhead if needed (see map).

The way we have taken through Holyhead may seem uninspiring but is chosen simply for safety, to avoid the A5. We wanted a route to pass the Roman Fort but the one-way system makes this difficult. If you choose to visit this site, you cannot avoid a right turn onto the A5, a stretch on it, and a right turn off it. With young children it is best not to do this but to follow the back street route as described. It soon leaves the town and heads for the open countryside. Although most of the route follows minor roads they can be busy in the height of the summer. They are quiet outside the tourist season. Residents or visitors could also start at Trearddur Bay.

THE RIDE

MAIN ROUTE 17 miles. Trearddur Bay Loop only, 10 miles

From the prom overlooking the harbour in **Holyhead** ride towards the harbour and take the first right signed Ynys Lawd/South Stack and Canolfan Ucheldre, into Walthew Avenue. Pass the playground. At the cross roads turn left and immediately right into Maes Cybi housing estate. Go to the end, turn left and pass a school, Carreglwyd. Pass the new Ucheldre Centre (converted church), a shop, the Chester pub. Keep right round the bend passing an area of terraced houses all with uniform pebbledashing and the Salem Chapel. Follow the left bend. At the T-junction opposite the English Methodist Church turn right and go straight on down Maeshyfryd Road. Turn second left by the telephone down Kings Road. At the T-junction by the National Tyre Centre turn right into the Old Post Road. This is the B4545 through the **Kingsland** area of Holyhead.

[If you have followed the one-way system instead and visited the Roman fort or if you have arrived by boat or train then join the route here by turning, **with great care**, into the B4545 by the railway bridge.]

Pass the Foresters Arms, a shop, a fish and chip shop, and the old Hebron Chapel and then climb a short hill. Turn left by the telephone into the one way Tyn Pwll Road. (Or if you need a cycle shop continue a few yards further on the B road and DRP Owen's Dorset Sports Stores is on the left.) Pass older stone cottages and at the cross roads go straight across by the Kingsland School into Maes Cyttir. The lane now leaves the houses behind and is quickly in beautiful open country.

Anglesey Aluminium is the remaining outpost of the present civilisation. You soon arrive at plenty of evidence of previous civilisations! *Tŷ-Mawr* standing stone dates from 2000-1500BC on the right. It may have been set up during the Early Bronze Age. A few yards further on the left is *Trefignath* Burial Chamber. It is not far to another standing stone on the right.

Soon on the left there is an inlet of the sea from the east side of the island, even though we are less than ½ mile from the west coast. Leave Lon Towyn Capel at the T-junction by turning left onto the B4545 by the Towyn stores. Decide here whether to do the Extra Loop to Rhoscolyn.

To continue on the Main Loop turn immediately right, **with care**, to the beach at Trearddur Bay and follow instructions from * later.

EXTRA LOOP TO RHOSCOLYN 7½ miles

Follow the signs for Dyffryn/Valley for a couple of miles on the B road towards Four Mile Bridge. The road goes through Trearddur Bay first. Pass shops, cafes, toilets, the Beach Hotel, post office, a church and of course several chapels. There is a derelict windmill visible over the fields. Pass another inlet of the sea on the left, a chapel and then the Anchorage Hotel. Then at Y Gegin Fach cafe turn right signed Rhoscolyn opposite Sardis Chapel (1828). It is about 1½ miles down to Rhoscolyn from here. Four Mile Bridge and the Valley Lakes Link to Ride 11 would be reached if you carried straight on the main road.

It is a really good ride along this lane through wild open country with a mixture of pasture and bog and usually plenty of birds to watch. Continue straight on past a left turn for Silver Bay Caravan Park. Then just past Rhoscolyn Church Hall, at the fork take the left one, signed White Eagle Inn, for the diversion to the beach—a must despite the later ascent! It is a pleasant gentle glide down this winding narrow lane, passing the inn. You could leave the bikes secured by the toilets to explore Porth Wen on foot.

It is a wonderful beach—one of my firm favourites with clean sand, rocky outcrops and sheltered safe swimming at high water. There are good views to the headlands and the lifeboat house as well as distant views to the Lleyn and its mountains. It even has a European Community Clean Beach Award. I don't think that the arrangement of standing stones in the field is genuinely old.

Retrace your route back up the lane, passing the pub, to the fork and turn left. Then keep right by the church of St Gwenfaen. It is a lovely ride for 1½ miles along this rural lane.

At the T-junction turn left onto the B4545. Pass the Old Turnpike Cottage. It is about a mile retracing your outward route back to Trearddur Bay. Pass the Beach Hotel. You can reach the beach at several points eg down Ravenspoint Road, or a little further and left through the car park. There is a concrete prom round the top of the beach. Or continue on the road a little further and turn next left. The Main Route rejoins * here by the Waterfront cafe and Trearddur Bay Hotel.

MAIN ROUTE continued...
There is good sand, clean water, rocky islets and plenty of facilities for a spot of holidaymaking here. A good place to picnic or at least sample the ice cream. There is usually a stall selling hot drinks and snacks as well. It also has a European Clean Beach designation.

Continue northwestwards along the coast. This is a splendid coastal ride but is rather hilly as we follow the cliff top. It is subject to winds, being open to the Atlantic Ocean! (The waves can be absolutely enormous in winter storms—there's plenty of uninterrupted ocean to build up their height as the next stop is Ireland or in one direction America!) Pass the Cliff Hotel. Drop down to Porth y Post, then climb, then drop steeply down to Porth Dafarch. If you are continuing it is worth maintaining a safe speed to help you up the next ascent. There is a Short Cut back from the cove.

SHORT CUT 2 miles back
Turn right at Porth Dafarch into Porth Dafarch Road. Pass a standing stone on the left and follow this narrow lane through pleasant countryside for about a mile back to the Kingsland area. Turn left by the Forester's Arms and the Angel onto the B4545 and left onto the A5 **with care.**

Turn left again by the New Harbour Inn into Holborn Road. At the next T-junction turn right, passing the Methodist Church, and then onto the one way system in the centre of Holyhead. Go straight on at the Britannia into Thomas Street and then into Porth y Felin Road. At the main road turn right into Walthew Avenue to return to the prom.

MAIN ROUTE continued...
Continue up the steep hill from Porth Dafarch. There are phenomenal views—phew!—from the top. Pass a right turn at Penrhosfeilw which could be another slightly shorter inland route back.

After a mile turn left for a there-and-back **detour** if you wish to visit **South Stack**. This road can be busy with tourist traffic at peak periods.

To continue keep straight on beneath Holyhead Mountain. We have good views up to the hill: it is a beautiful purple and gold in late summer with heather and gorse. Pass a pond with swans, then a few houses, a chapel called Seilo and Y Ddraig Goch (the Red Dragon) pub. Then decide on the Off-Road or Road Route.

OFF-ROAD ROUTE 1½ miles
After the sharp right bend turn second left by Lôn Cae Serri retirement bungalows. Turn left and ride uphill to the end where there is a view ahead to Soldiers' Point and the cliffs, as well as the Breakwater Country Park Visitor Centre. We then leave the road. If you can get your bike through the kissing gate ahead or if you can carry it over, you could reach the Visitor Centre on a newly widened path (give way to pedestrians). If not, or if you fancy something muddier, turn right. It is necessary to dismount for a short way unless you are very intrepid and on a mountain bike! It is steeply down on a very rocky track. At the bottom bear right along a narrow path. Give way to pedestrians and dismount if necessary. It isn't possible to rejoin the road at the first bridge; there is no way down. Continue along the path and at the second bridge there is an access track down.

After either way down, turn right onto the road, which follows a disused railway in a cutting through the Country Park. Pass an information board and the Boathouse Hotel. Turn right at the end onto the prom and follow it back to the start.

Breakwater Country Park

ROAD ROUTE 1 mile
Stay on the road after the Red Dragon and continue for ½ mile into the outskirts of Holyhead. Turn left by the tennis courts into New Park Road, which becomes Walthew Avenue and leads back down to the prom.

LINK FROM RIDE 10 TO 11 7 miles
'The Valley Lakes Link'
¾ mile along the B4545 from Four Mile Bridge towards Valley turn right, **with care**, by the level crossing into a minor lane which is flat at first. Cross the estuary and climb slightly. Turn first left over the railway bridge. Continue for ½ mile on a somewhat grassy lane. At the T-junction turn right. After ¾ mile go over the railway bridge and turn left onto a wider road. You soon reach the reed fringed lake **Llyn Cerrig Bach**. Pass the Valley Airfield and turn sharp left over the bridge. Pass **Llyn Penrhyn** and cycle through Llanfihangel yn Nhowyn. At the end of the village turn right beneath two runway beacons onto a narrow lane. After a mile, cross a narrow bridge (weight limit 7½ tons) over a pretty stream, the Afon Crigyll. Go straight across the next crossroads. After another mile just past a sharp

right bend turn next right and into the minor lane (before the chicken farm). You are then at ++ in Ride 11.

OTHER INFORMATION

HOLYHEAD/CAERGYBI

Tourist Information Centre *is near the port entrance and is open from 9.30-5 Monday to Saturday, tel 01407 762622. The Ucheldre Centre is off Millbank and we pass it. It has a programme of events, exhibitions and club activities. There is a craft shop, music shop and kitchen selling light refreshments. It is open from 10-5 weekdays and 2-5 Sundays, tel 01407 763361.*

The church of **St Cybi** *is in the town centre and on the site of a 6th century church built within the Roman walls of the 3rd century* **Roman fort**. *Don't spend too long looking for the door to the fort, the archaeologists can't find it either!*

The Triumphal Arch *was built in 1821 to commemorate the visit of George IV as a duplicate of Marble Arch in London—at the other end of the A5. You knew you had reached the very end of the A5 when you arrived at the arch! The port is busy with passenger and cargo boats to and from Dun Laoghaire. Packet boats to the republic sailed from as early as 1573.*

The route we take through Kingsland is that of the old coach road, which was once an important route for travellers from London to Ireland. It is called Old Post Road through this area.

Trefignath Burial Chamber *is Neolithic dating from about 3000BC and was used for communal burials. Tall stones mark the entrance. Like the others on Anglesey it was originally covered with a mound of stones which can be seen scattered round it. It comprises three chambers in which pottery and tools have been found. It is most impressive, particularly if you imagine what conditions may have been and how the people moved and arranged the stones.*

Holyhead Mountain *is Mynydd Twr in Welsh. It is the highest point on Anglesey at 220 metres. When it is clear you can, if you are lucky, see both the Isle of Man and the mountains of Mourne in Ireland. The summit was an ancient fortress and there may have been a lighthouse here even in Roman times.*

Ellin's Tower Seabird Centre *is an RSPB reserve on the South Stack cliffs. The tower is a restored folly and gives a wonderful view to the cliffs where the seabirds build their precarious nests in Spring. Entry is free. It is open from Easter to September from 11-5 daily.*

South Stack lighthouse *was built in 1809 and is automatic. Its tower is 28 metres high and its height is 60 metres above Mean High Water with a range of 28 miles and a power of 2½ million candela. It used to be open to the public and it was a scary crossing over the chain bridge to reach it. There is a discussion at present* about reopening it. You can still climb down the many steps but there is no longer access to the island. It is worth the climb for the better view and to see the rocks, birds and plants. There are weird folds in the rocks. It is wonderful for bird watching in Spring, especially for puffins, razorbills, guillemots and little auks. Choughs can be seen and heard all year!

HOLYHEAD BREAKWATER COUNTRY PARK
The Breakwater is the longest in the UK. It was built in 1845-73. Its light is 70 feet above high water level. The country park has recently been designated to include the land around here up to the derelict quarry and much work is being carried out on landscaping and providing interpretation of features of interest. There are new car parks, a visitor centre and toilets. Most of the new stiles are well designed for cyclists. Warden tel 01407 760530.

The Skerries Lighthouse can be seen from here. It was built in 1714 by William Trench. In 1987 it was converted to automatic. Its range is 29 miles and intensity 4 million candela.

TREARDDUR BAY
This means 'homestead of Iarddur' (an old Welsh family name). Saint Ffraid, the patron saint of the area, was famous for her supposed miraculous powers and had a chapel in the centre of the bay. It is a wonderful sandy beach, with interesting rocky outcrops, ideal for bathing and watersports.

Porth Dafarch and Porth y Post are both tiny sandy coves near Trearddur which are also good for swimming if Trearddur is busy. Nearby are two impressive standing stones at Penrhosfeilw, easy to miss if you are maintaining speed on the descent to the cove ready for the next ascent! Beakers left by the 'Beaker People' have been found at Porth Dafarch.

FOUR MILE BRIDGE/PONT RHYD-BONT
Before Telford's bridge, people crossed to Holy Island by the sands here. There was a shipbuilding industry and trade in lime, timber, coal and salt. Ynys Halen or Salt Island here is named from the salt workings. Sea water was left to evaporate and salt was left.

PENRHOS COASTAL PARK/PARC GLANNAU PENRHOS
This is a nature reserve owned and managed by Anglesey Aluminium. The estate was previously owned by the Stanley family of Alderley from 1763. It is part of a designated Area of Outstanding Natural Beauty. It was opened to the public in 1972 under the wardenship of Ken Williams, a retired policeman and well known local naturalist. There are woodland and coastal walks with good views. Soon there will be a cycleway through here to avoid the main road. Cycling is permitted on coastal and roadside routes only. There are stiles and kissing gates on some footpaths. There is a cafe in the restored Telford Toll House and a small

interpretative centre open most days between April and September from 11-3, tel 01407 760949

RHOSCOLYN
Saint Gwenfaen's church was founded here in 6th century. It is a lovely cove and one of the best on the island for safe bathing. Marble quarried in the area was used for Worcester, Bristol and Peterborough cathedrals.

VALLEY LAKES
These are on the link from Ride 10 to 11. They are managed now by the RSPB centred at Llyn Penrhyn. Llyn Cerrig Bach was held to be a sacred lake by the Druids. Anglesey was a centre of European importance for this culture and the last stronghold of it. The Celts held territories from the 5th century BC until the Roman conquest. Much treasure has been found in the lake including bronze plates, chariots, swords, daggers, slave chains, spears, shells and cauldrons. They may have been offerings to the Celtic underworld.

THE PUBS
There are many in Holyhead.
The Beach Hotel in Trearddur Bay, which is a large hotel on the main road, and the Trearddur Bay Hotel both have restaurants and bar meals.
The White Eagle Inn at Rhoscolyn (free house) has a beer garden.
The Red Dragon/Y Ddraig Goch (Bass) bar snacks, children welcome, beer garden.
The Boathouse Hotel in Holyhead near the Country Park serves bar meals, morning coffee and afternoon tea. It overlooks the bay.

RIDE 11

ABERFFRAW TO RHOSNEIGR

<table>
<tr><td>ROUTE</td><td>Aberffraw—Dothan—Engedi—Capel Gwyn—
Rhosneigr—Bryn Du—Ty Croes—Aberffraw</td></tr>
<tr><td>DISTANCE</td><td>14 miles/22 km</td></tr>
<tr><td>ASCENT</td><td>120 metres. Gentle.</td></tr>
<tr><td>START</td><td>Llys Llewelyn Visitor Centre at Aberffraw, Grid Ref
354691.</td></tr>
<tr><td>TO START</td><td>Take the B4422 off the A5 or the A4080 round the
coast to Aberffraw.</td></tr>
</table>

This is a lovely ride with several beaches with both sand and rocks. For contrast there are also fields with small streams. The lanes are mostly very quiet and the terrain is flat.

THE RIDE

MAIN ROUTE 14 miles

From the Llys Llewelyn Visitor Centre in Aberffraw pass the Prince Llewelyn pub. Turn left onto the main road, and immediately right **with care**. It is a straight, flat lane for 1½ miles and is a very pleasant part of the route. Go under the railway and straight on through Glanrafon for ½ mile. There are then views to the left over Llyn Padrig, a very shallow marshy lake. On your right pass the old chapel with a tiny bell. After a mile there is a stony outcrop in the field on the right at Cerrig Cafael.

Turn left at the cross roads (by a telephone) and go downhill for ½ mile to Dothan. Fork right and Dothan chapel is visible down to the left dating from 1902. Continue downhill for ½ mile then fork left onto a very narrow lane which has grass down the middle. Pass a chapel and Ty Croes farm and continue up the hill with impressive views behind to the mountains of Snowdonia and ahead to Holyhead Mountain. Go under the pylons and straight on to reach the main road at Engedi opposite a converted chapel. Go straight across the A4080, **with care**.

Pass a large chicken farm and then turn first left, just before a right hand

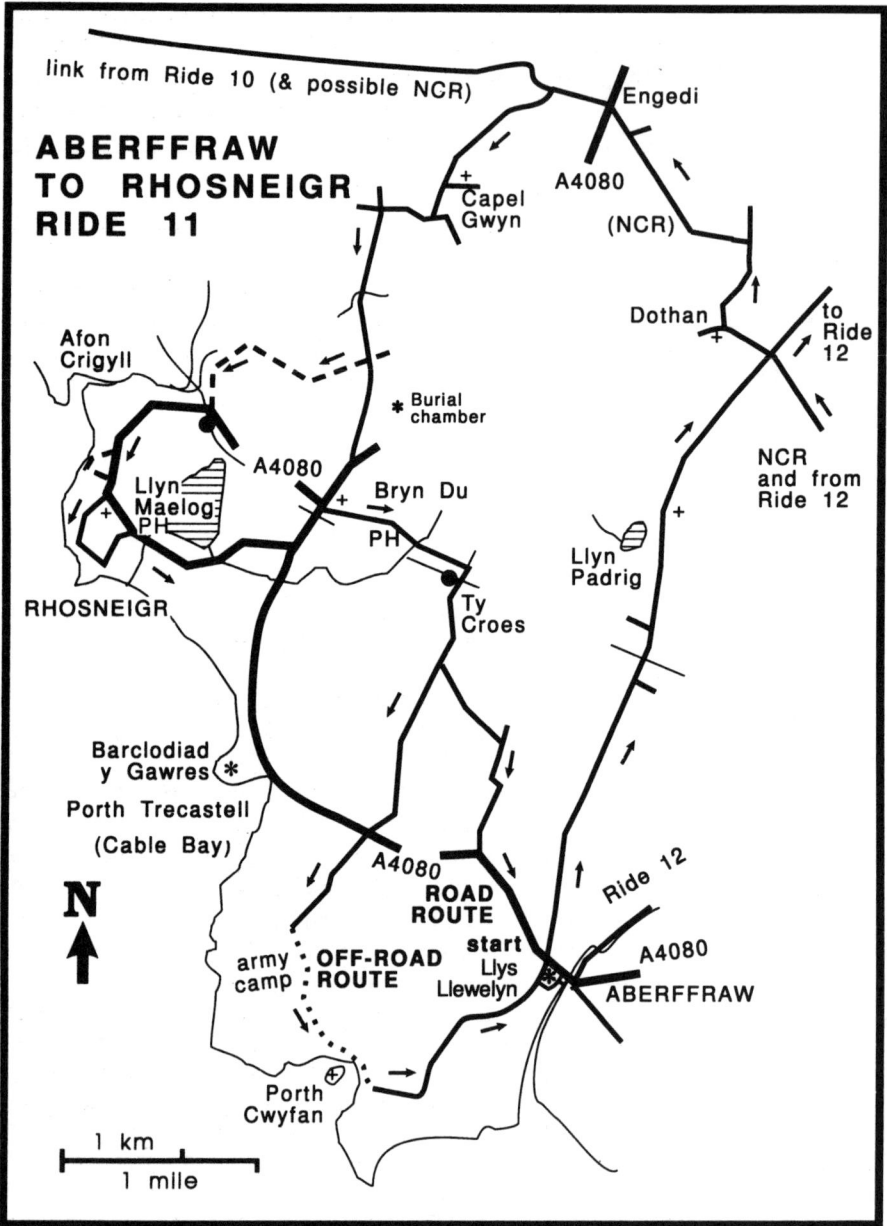

ABERFFRAW TO RHOSNEIGR RIDE 11

link from Ride 10 (& possible NCR)

Engedi

Capel Gwyn

A4080 (NCR)

Dothan

to Ride 12

NCR and from Ride 12

Afon Crigyll

Burial chamber

A4080

Llyn Maelog
PH

Bryn Du

PH

Ty Croes

Llyn Padrig

RHOSNEIGR

Barclodiad y Gawres

Porth Trecastell (Cable Bay)

A4080

ROAD ROUTE

Ride 12

N

army camp

OFF-ROAD ROUTE

start
Llys Llewelyn

A4080
ABERFFRAW

Porth Cwyfan

1 km

1 mile

bend, not down the gated lane. ++ **Link Rides 10-11 'Valley Lakes Link' joins here.** Cycle along the narrow lane. It is a mile on this secluded byway to Capel Gwyn. Turn right at the large house with a post box set in its wall (just beyond is Capel Gwyn 1905). The lane has a better surface but is still interestingly winding. After ¼ mile keep right round the bend and in ¼ mile turn left at the cross roads.

After 1 mile almost at the top of the hill at a tiny crossroads turn right onto a gravelly track. It is about a mile, mainly downhill, to a little valley containing reedbeds and a stream which meanders through the salt marsh. You may be lucky enough to see nesting swans and grazing horses. At the A4080 turn right, **with care**, and go under the railway bridge by the station. Pass the golf club and enter the outskirts of **Rhosneigr.**

Holiday Cycling

Turn right by the corner shop onto a lane which winds between the older houses in the original part of the town. Go onto a sandy track which leads to the ruins of the once imposing Bay Hotel. This leads to the beach, an excellent place for a rest or a picnic. There isn't much tranquillity, however, as there are frequent noisy aircraft from RAF Valley. The beach is named Traeth Crigyll after the Afon Crigyll which has its estuary here.

Go up past the Bay Hotel on your left (beware of broken glass) to the Minstrel Lodge Hotel. Turn right to the centre of Rhosneigr **with care** as this area can be busy in summer. Pass the clock tower and turn slightly (not sharp) right between the two banks. Pass a chip shop, a cafe, several other shops, village hall and chapel. Go down to the end of High Street and along the edge of the bay. There are several ways down to the beach here for alternative picnic stops.

Continue past many newer houses and bungalows until just past Bryn Maelog Guest House turn right and then at the T-junction turn right **with care** onto the main road. Opposite is the Cefn Dref pub. The route now passes **Llyn Maelog** and there are lovely views over the lake. Off to the right is the Llyn Maelog Hotel. Continue to the T-junction with the main road, the A4080.

SHORT CUT
Turn right **with care** and follow the main road back for about 3 miles to Aberffraw. This isn't a busy road except during the height of the summer. It has the bonus of passing two lovely beaches at Porth Nobla and Porth Trecastell (Cable Bay).

MAIN ROUTE continued...
To continue turn left, cross the railway and in ¼ mile turn first right **with care** in Llanfaelog. Pass the church of St Maelog and follow the sign Ty Croes station. Pass a derelict windmill, old buildings and a chapel dating from 1901. Ride down to a tiny pub in **Bryn Du** called the Queen's Head. At the railway station turn right and go over the level crossing. Decide on whether to follow the Off-Road Route or not.

ROAD ROUTE...
In ½ mile turn left and go down to the main road after a mile by the house with a very large barn. Turn left towards Aberffraw. Turn right at the Prince Llewelyn and the Visitor Centre is first on the right in **Aberffraw**.

OFF-ROAD ROUTE 2 miles further *(includes off-road and a walk)*
Cycle straight on for 1½ miles to the main road. Go straight across signed 'Private Road for Farms only and Ty Croes Range'. Go towards the old army camp but turn left down the stony track (a public footpath). After passing a farm the track bends and becomes even more rough!

It isn't far to the sea where you are rewarded with splendid views of Church Island. It is possible to walk out to it when the tide is out. Walk across the top of the stony beach along the footpath to the road. Go up the narrow lane (on tarmac again). It is about a mile to the village. Go along Church Street and into the square. Opposite the shop is the very narrow street which leads back to the Visitor Centre.

OTHER INFORMATION

ABERFFRAW

Aberffraw has a long and important place in Welsh history. It was invaded by the Vikings in AD 968. Between the 7th and 13th centuries Aberffraw was the capital of the principality of Gwynedd. The palace was in the centre of the present village. A Norman arch reset in the church of St Beuno is believed to be from the palace. There were 9 buildings for the king within the llys (court) including a hall, refectory, kitchen, sleeping quarters, toilet and brewhouse! Archaeologists have revealed traces of the wall and ditch or moat round the oldest part of the village. The private mill on the river was a water mill for centuries.

LLYS LLEWELYN VISITOR CENTRE

There are informative displays, as well as toilets and a cafe. It is the headquarters of Anglesey Coastal Heritage and is open from 1st April from Tuesday to Saturday 11-5 and Sunday 1-5, tel 01407 840845.

RHOSNEIGR & LLYN MAELOG

*It is believed that the name means 'moor of the adder' and we have certainly seen several adders both large and small basking in the sun on the cliff paths around here and Aberffraw. The church of St Maelog is one of the oldest on the island having been founded in 605. There was once shipbuilding on the shores of the lake but now **Llyn Maelog** is a haven for birds disturbed only by the windsurfers. It was until recently a beautiful clean lake but now sampling by my students shows farm slurry pollution coming in from the stream to the east. Let us hope that the aquatic life on which the fish and birds depend can survive until this problem is rectified. The Afon Crigyll or Crugyll enters the sea at Rhosneigr. The name comes from Crug, meaning cairn or burial chamber. Traeth Crigyll was renowned for the infamous wreckers who used to lure ships to their doom and then reap their unjust rewards from the shipwrecks. Today it is a beautiful and peaceful place, ideal for a beach picnic! At the southern side is the locally named Broad Beach backed by sand dunes and with the Lion Rocks at the far end.*

PORTH TRECASTELL/CABLE BAY

*This can only be reached by bike on the main road. A better way to visit is on foot by the footpath from the southern end of Rhosneigr. The English name refers to the transatlantic cable which goes under the sea to America from here. The impressive Neolithic burial mound called **Barclodiad y Gawres** or 'the giantess's apronful' is on the headland. Its name refers to the Welsh legend that a giantess spilled her apronful of stones here. It contains stone pillars decorated with carvings.*

LLANGWYFAN

The church is on the tiny island at Porth Cwyfan and is named after Saint Cwyfan. The nave and chancel were built in the 12th century, the doorway in the 15th and the rest in the 14th. In 1846 the walls of the island were destroyed by the sea and graves were being washed away so the walls were rebuilt. The cliff top walk from Porth Cwyfan to Aberffraw is splendid and the rock pools are full of interesting marine life.

THE PUBS

Y Goron and The Prince Llewelyn (both Burtonwood) are both in Aberffraw. Queens Head (Burtonwood) in Bryn Du has a beer garden with free range hens!

RIDE 12

ABERFFRAW TO LLYN CORON AND GWALCHMAI

ROUTE	First Loop, Aberffraw—Llyn Coron—Soar—Llangadwaladr—Hermon—Aberffraw dunes. Second Loop, Soar—Gwalchmai—Hen Blas detour—Bethel—rejoin First Loop. Extra Loop on Second Loop, Capel Mawr—Malltraeth marsh—Glantraeth—Bethel—rejoin First Loop
DISTANCE	15 miles/24 km. First Loop, 8 miles. Second Loop, 8 miles. Or Second Loop + Extra Loop, 10½ miles.
ASCENT	160 metres. Gentle. One ascent on Extra Loop.
START	Llys Llewelyn Visitor Centre at Aberffraw, Grid Ref 354691.
TO START	Take the B4422 off the A5 or the A4080 round the coast to Aberffraw.

The First Loop is really good, the Second is fairly good but has 1½ miles on a B road and the Extra Loop is interesting but has a short climb. There is an off-road track to cross a stream near Llyn Coron and another across the Afon Gwna. This ride is designed with 'bolt on' extra sections to use the current jargon! The idea being that you can chose the length of route desired more easily and do variations. The Second Loop only omits 1 mile of the First between Soar and Bethel. The whole is done clockwise as none of the right turns is particularly problematical. For extra length you can link with Rides 11 or 13 or even the projected National Cycle Route.

THE RIDE
FIRST LOOP 8 miles
From the Llys Llewelyn Visitor Centre ride out of the main gate and straight on for a few yards into the square. Opposite is a shop selling ice cream and soft drinks. Go diagonally past Y Goron and ride steeply downhill (passing a drinking water supply issuing out of a lion's head) to the old packhorse bridge. Cross the river Ffraw by this bridge, fork left and reach the A4080.

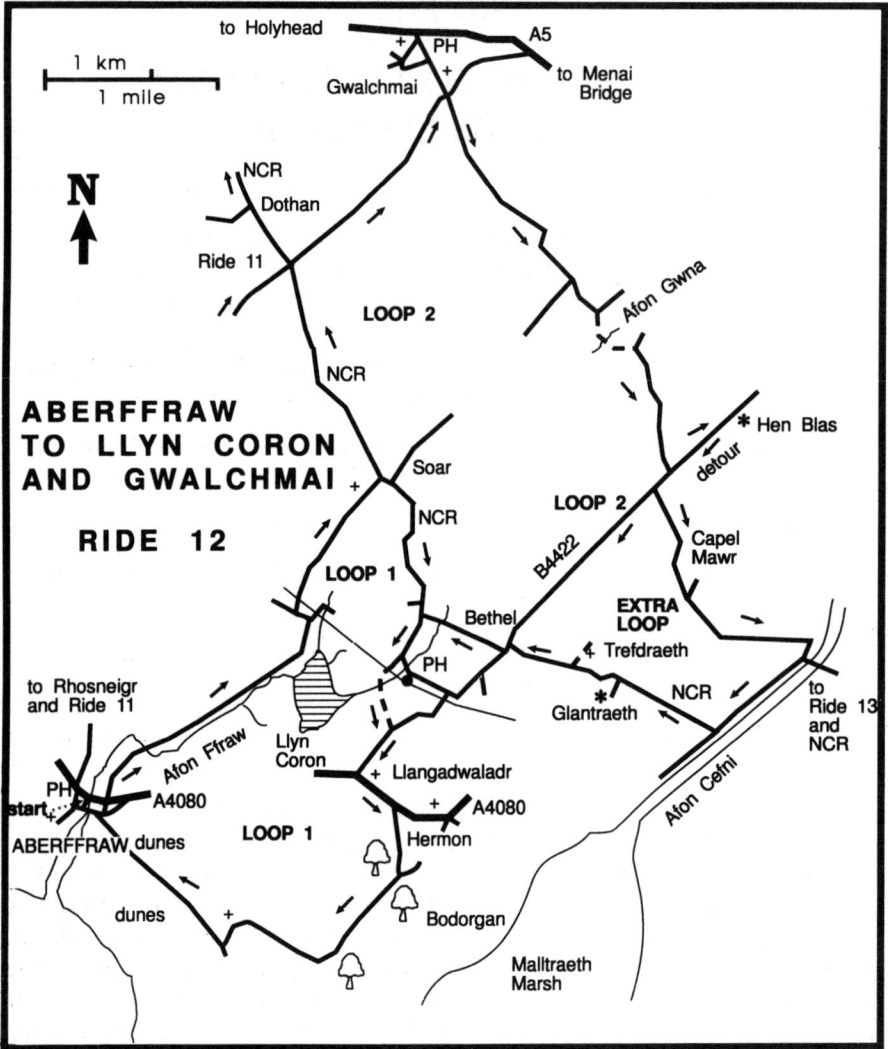

ABERFFRAW
TO LLYN CORON
AND GWALCHMAI

RIDE 12

Cross over the road onto an unsigned narrow lane. Cross the fast flowing Afon Ffraw again by an old bridge. There is now a delightful 1½ miles along this lane which follows the Afon Ffraw. There are pleasant open views over the gorse-clad old dunes to the distant hills. There is often much wildlife to be seen when you are cycling quietly. Stonechats and larks serenade you in summer. There are marshes as well as glimpses of **Llyn Coron**. Turn left just before the railway and then in a few yards first right under it. There are many primroses, bluebells, lady's smock, celandine and violets in the hedgebanks in spring.

It is 1 mile to **Soar** chapel dated 1872. Decide whether to continue onto Loop 2 or whether to return on Loop 1. For Loop 1 only: turn right in Soar and follow the winding lane for just over a mile and see * in text to continue.

SECOND LOOP 8 miles
At the T-junction in **Soar** turn left and cycle for 1¼ miles to a crossroads. This crossroads forms the **link with Ride 11**. Turn right by the telephone. Continue for 1½ miles to **Gwalchmai**. Here is a shop, Pen y Groes, selling ice creams and soft drinks but it is closed at present on weekend afternoons.

If you need refreshments, the alternative is to turn left and cycle downhill past the chapel and turn right into the back of the car park of the Gwalchmai. Then either visit the pub or walk across the main road, **with care,** to the Shell Garage shop. Return uphill to the crossroads and go straight across, or turn right here if you omitted the detour. There are good views of the distant mountains of Snowdonia from this lane. Go straight on for 1½ miles and go under pylons. Then go straight on where a road turns off right (this would make a quieter but less interesting return to Soar).

Go straight on at the farm with the corrugated iron barn into a very narrow lane which has grass down the middle. All the lanes round here have ditches full of interesting pondweeds and wildlife. There is a view of a castellated mansion on a rocky hillock to your left. After ½ mile turn right at the T-junction and follow this winding lane for almost a mile to the B4422. Here you can turn left for a short detour to visit **Hen Blas** (½ mile each way).

Turn right, **with care,** onto the main road and in only a few yards decide whether to do the Extra Loop to Capel Mawr and Glantraeth. To omit this, simply continue along the B4422 for 1½ miles to **Bethel**. This can be busy. Turn right and descend for ½ mile to a T-junction, turn left and see * later.

EXTRA LOOP extra 2½ miles, making 10½ miles for Loop 2
Turn immediately first left signed **Capel Mawr**. Follow the bendy road and

pass a graveyard. Go steeply downhill (test brakes first), then straight then wiggly! Bend right before **Pont Marquis** and follow the water. This mile is in common with the Newborough Ride but is in the opposite direction. It is so good for cycling, it is well worth doing again and again. Turn first right signed **Glantraeth** Restaurant and Animal Farm. Climb uphill to the T-junction in **Bethel** and turn left. Either turn first right (or see + for the station) onto a pleasant lane which descends for ½ mile to a T-junction where you turn left.

(+ Or, if you want the station turn next right onto a quiet lane which goes past the Meyrick Arms Hotel and **Bodorgan** station. Continue as far as the next sharp bend.)

All routes recombine here *.

Cycling on quiet roads

Turn left from the direction of Bodorgan Station or right from all other directions onto a 9ft 9in wide cart track lined with hawthorns—be warned! It is unsuitable for motor vehicles but splendid on a bike! Go downhill for ¼ mile, past abandoned old houses to the stream. There is a pool made by a small dam in the stream which makes a good picnic spot. Either walk over the old bridge or cycle through the ford. Climb gently uphill for ½ mile again being wary of hawthorns. There are many wild flowers and two footpaths lead off to Llyn Coron.

At the T-junction turn right, **with care**. It is ¼ mile to the A4080. The old church of **Llangadwaladr** is by the junction and is well worth a visit. Turn left and follow the main road for only ¼ mile to turn first right, **with care**, in Hermon. Climb up through the old woods and admire the ancient pine and yew. The ground is carpeted with ferns such as harts tongue and male ferns. There only seems to be one patch of bluebells in the spring. At the imposing gateway of the private Bodorgan estate turn right at the T-junction. It is now about 2 miles of mainly downhill gliding—delightful! After passing Beulah Chapel (1879) the road crosses the dunes. It follows a tiny ditch and it is well worth doing this ride in spring to see the profusion of wild flowers. Please remember that they are protected and must not be picked. Also don't cycle on the dunes as this causes irreparable erosion: stick to the road—end of lecture and almost end of ride!

On reaching the river you could walk along it to the beach—ideal for a picnic. Turn left over the ancient packhorse bridge and cycle up into the town of **Aberffraw**. Go into the square, past Y Goron and right to return to the Visitor Centre at the end.

OTHER INFORMATION

ABERFFRAW AND LLYS LLEWELYN VISITOR CENTRE See Ride 11

LLANGADWALADR

Although the village is very small the church was important as it was dedicated to Cadwaladr who, in the 7th century, was the last king to rule over a united Britain for a long time. It was another thousand years before Britain was one again. He is portrayed in a stained glass window dating from the 15th century. Cadwaladr placed an inscribed stone here in the 7th century telling of his grandfather Cadfan as being 'the wisest and most illustrious of kings' in a Latin inscription. This was carved in 640 AD and is therefore the oldest memorial to a king in Western Europe.

HEN BLAS

This is a 230 acre country park claiming the largest indoor play area in North Wales. The main house dates from the 15th century and the tithe barn from the 18th. There are rare breeds, shire horses, cart rides, picnic sites, nature trails and a neolithic burial chamber. This dolmen is interesting as it is made of Gwna quartzite and the lines under the top stone indicate that this huge stone has been turned both over and round. Hen Blas has an exhibition, tea room and gift shop. It is open from Whit to October daily from 10.30-5 (last admission 4) and less often at other times, tel 01407 840229 or 840152.

GLANTRAETH
The Animal Park has a small admission charge. Open Tuesday to Saturday from 11-5.30, closed Mondays except Bank Holidays.

GWALCHMAI
This is really two small villages. There are remnants of an old windmill and watermill. This was the first village on the island to have electric lights! There is an old Toll House on the A5 which was designed by Telford. The Anglesey Agricultural Show is held annually on fields nearby.

LLYN CORON
This is private and access is restricted round most of the shore but on the north side there is a short footpath to the lakeside just beyond our ford crossing. If you are a keen bird watcher it is worth visiting in winter to see a good variety of swans, geese and ducks including ruddy ducks as well as perhaps, if you are lucky, great crested grebes, snipe, curlew, and golden plover. In summer you may be able to spot warblers, redshanks, moorhens, coots and stonechats. The Afon Gwna feeds the lake and the Afon Ffraw drains it. The name Gwna may came from Gwter Fudr meaning dirty gutter! The more pleasantly named Ffraw means flow of a stream (like the Frome in England).

THE PUBS
Y Goron and The Prince Llewelyn are in Aberffraw
The Gwalchmai (Ansells) in Gwalchmai serves bar meals
The Meyrick Arms Hotel (Murphy's Stout) at Bodorgan station serves bar meals.

RIDE 13

NEWBOROUGH FOREST
AND MALLTRAETH MARSH

ROUTE Newborough Forest—Llanddwyn Beach—
Malltraeth—Afon Cefni—Pont Marquis—Llangaffo—
Dwyran—Llangeinwen—Newborough

DISTANCE 14 miles/22 km. Short Cut 7 miles.

ASCENT 120 metres. Flat apart from two short hills.

START Newborough. Small free car park a few yards down
the road to the beach, Grid Ref 423657. Or FC paying
car park at the end of this road.

TO START A4080 from Llanfairpwll to Newborough. Turn left in
village signed the beach.

The route through the forest is really one of the best off-road rides in
Anglesey. There are about 6 miles off road. This is more tiring than cycling
on tarmac. The surfaces vary from gravel to sand. Allow plenty of time
especially with children. There are many access points to the beach but
please avoid the sand dunes to protect them and their wildlife from erosion.
Avoid riding on the verges of the tracks as again this would destroy the
wild flowers. There is very little climbing. The main hill is a steep one up
into Llangaffo which you miss if you do the Short Cut. If visiting the tourist
attractions in the Llangeinwen area be careful when cycling on the main
road.

THE RIDE

MAIN ROUTE 14 miles

From the crossroads on the A4080 in the centre of Newborough turn
towards the beach, Traeth Llanddwyn. There is a small public car park a
few yards down on the right. Pass Eglwys St Pedr (St Peter's Church) and
ride along the winding lane following the signs for the beach. Enter Forestry
Commission land (motorists pay at automatic barrier, free for cyclists) and
ride over a few 'sleeping policemen'. Turn first left along the bridleway
signposted with a horseshoe—this is easy to miss.

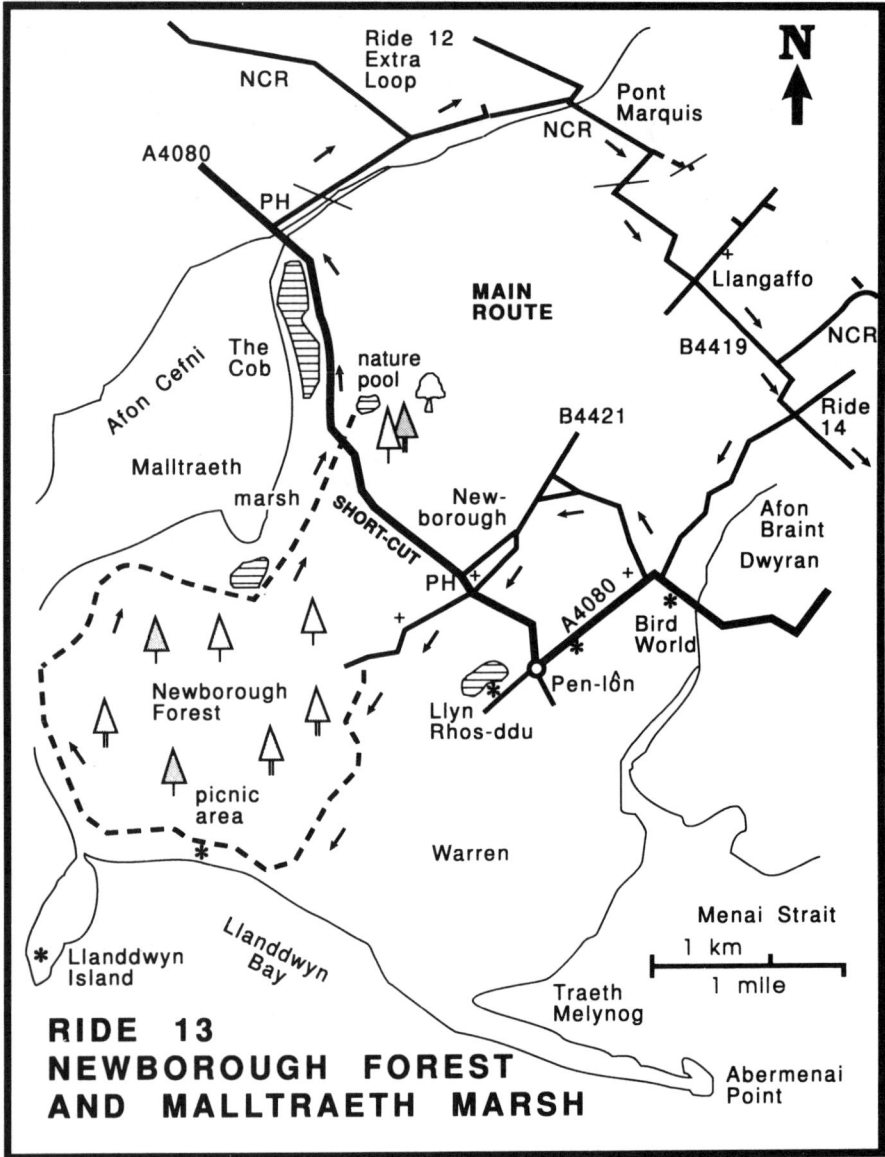

N

NCR

Ride 12
Extra Loop

Pont Marquis

NCR

A4080

PH

Llangaffo

MAIN ROUTE

B4419

NCR

Afon Cefni

The Cob

nature pool

Ride 14

Malltraeth

marsh

SHORT-CUT

B4421

New-borough

Afon Braint
Dwyran

PH

A4080

Bird World

Newborough Forest

Llyn Rhos-ddu

Pen-lôn

picnic area

Warren

Menai Strait

1 km

1 mile

Llanddwyn Island

Llanddwyn Bay

Traeth Melynog

Abermenai Point

RIDE 13
NEWBOROUGH FOREST
AND MALLTRAETH MARSH

Follow the track through the forest (do not follow the bridleway where it turns right on a grassy path), straight on for about 1 mile until the track bends and passes a lovely picnic spot in a clearing. The entrance to the beach is a short way further on; to the right is the huge FC car park and toilets.

Go around the car park and then turn first left signed Forest Walk/Rhodfa'r Goedwig (red 1m, green 2½ m). After ½ mile turn right at a T-junction following the horseshoe symbol again and pink waymark stumps. At the barrier go left (through a gap on its left) and follow the pink paint on stumps. Turn left by the bench leaving the horseshoe signs behind. This path is narrower and is very sandy. It may be necessary to walk for a few yards occasionally! Go through a slightly more open area with smaller trees (pass a yucca) and eventually come out into the open by Malltraeth Marsh. There is always standing water here but the puddles are shallow and not too bad for cycling through.

The track bends inland through the forest again and becomes gravelled. At the T-junction turn left and follow the horseshoes again on a better track to the main road at the edge of the forest. Opposite is Llyn Natur/Wildlife Pool, worth a short visit.

SHORT CUT 7 miles total
Turn right, **with care**, onto the A4080 and it is only 1 mile back to Newborough village to end the ride.

MAIN ROUTE continued...
Turn left and follow the main road past the pool created by the embankment (the Cob), with shelduck, coots, swans and waders, and the open marshy area of the Malltraeth sands. Both the pool and marsh are excellent for bird watching, especially in winter. Cross the Afon Cefni (the Joiners Arms is visible ahead). Turn right immediately and follow the river. It is a wonderful ride for a mile and a half on a quiet, totally flat lane with views of the water. The route passes a turn to the Glantraeth restaurant and then goes under the railway and this mile is in common with the Extra Loop on Ride 12. Turn right and cross the river by Pont Marquis. Follow the winding narrow lane beside a small stream with marsh marigolds and water plantain.

Continue on the surfaced lane under the railway and then up a short but very steep hill. There is plenty of opportunity to admire the trees and wild flowers while climbing slowly! There are ash, elder, hawthorn, gorse, sloe and sycamore with campion, chickweed, dock, plantain, knapweed, polypody and harts tongue ferns.

At the cross roads in Llangaffo go straight across the B4421, **with care**. Follow the lane opposite the shop downhill to cross a tiny stream and then steeply uphill to turn first right at a cross roads. (This point links with Ride 14.) It is a very attractive narrow lane for a mile just above the Afon Braint with the village of Dwyran on the far side of the valley. At the T-junction with the A4080 turn right, **with care**, (better to get off and walk the few yards rather than crossing the road with children) and turn immediately first right just before the church of Llangeinwein.

In holiday gear

DETOURS

To visit Anglesey Bird World turn left onto the main road. It is only a couple of hundred yards on your right. It is safer to return to the Main Route for the return. Or to visit The Model Village turn right, **with care**, onto the main road at Llangeinwen. It is about ½ mile. You could then continue, **with care**, on this straight section of main road to the roundabout at Pen-lôn. There is a bird-hide down the lane on the left here. To return to Newborough cycle back to the roundabout, turn left for ½ mile gently uphill back to the village.

MAIN ROUTE continued...

Go uphill for ½ mile along the narrow lane and after a left bend take the left fork. Turn left onto the B4421 and after ½ mile you reach the centre of Newborough. Turn left amongst the houses and pass public toilets and a post office. At the cross roads there is a fish and chip shop on the right and opposite is the White Lion pub. Go straight across towards Traeth Llanddwyn beach and return to the car park a few yards on the right.

OTHER INFORMATION

NEWBOROUGH FOREST, WARREN, LLANDDWYN BAY AND ISLAND

The National Nature Reserve covers about 1500 acres and is one of the largest expanses of sand dunes in western Britain. There is a great variety of habitats and an interesting succession of wildlife communities from the mobile dunes to fixed dunes as well as dune slack vegetation and scrub. It is a haven for wildlife and a wonderful place to visit and explore provided you keep to the rights of way and avoid any risk to the plants and animals (such as marram, dewberry, stonecrop, storksbill, violets, spurge, silverweed and restharrow). Wild animals in the forest include squirrels, rabbits and cross-bills, and the plants: evening primrose, viper's bugloss and round leaved wintergreen are all of special interest.

The estuaries of the rivers Braint and Cefni and their salt marshes are found here and are good for bird watching. Llanddwyn Island has a beautiful coastline and its ancient pre-Cambrian rocks are of interest to geologists. Avoid disturbing the shingle-nesting terns at Whit. We have seen seals here in winter. One of the tiny fishermen's cottages has been restored and is open to the public. You can walk as far as the lighthouse from where there are excellent views down the Lleyn peninsula. The ruined priory was dedicated to Saint Dwynwen, the patron saint of lovers.

ANGLESEY BIRD WORLD

This has birds from around the world, tame water fowl, pets' corner, children's play area, miniature railway, refreshments and gift shop. It is open every day from 10-5.30, tel 01248 440627.

MODEL VILLAGE

This has scale models (1 inch:1 foot) of Anglesey buildings and countryside and a model railway. It is found on the A4080 in Dwyran a mile from Bird World and is open from Easter to October from 11.30-5. Admission charge, tel 01248 440477.

MALLTRAETH MARSH

The Afon Cefni is the major river on the island. The name Cefni means hollow or trough. The Cefni starts in the Cefni reservoir, goes through Llangefni and then flows through Malltraeth Marsh or Cors Ddyga to reach the sea via its huge estuary at Malltraeth Bay. The modern straight drainage channel takes the river by a different course to its original winding route. The marsh almost divided the island in half in the past. During a flood a few years back it almost did again. The sheep had taken refuge on tiny hummocks and were rescued by boat.

WILDLIFE POOL

There is a small car park, footpath around the lake and bird hide all hidden in the forest. So far there isn't very much bird life: presumably the aquatic life is still too sparse. It is best in spring when there are some young birds to see.

THE PUBS

The White Lion (Marstons) in Newborough.
The Joiners Arms (Free House) in Malltraeth. Bar Meals.

RIDE 14

BRYNSIENCYN, CHAMBERED CAIRNS AND THE SEA ZOO

ROUTE	Brynsiencyn—Llanidan—Llanddaniel Fab—Bryn Celli Ddu—Bodowyr—Dwyran—Sea Zoo—Brynsiencyn
DISTANCE	16 miles/26 km. Short Cut, 10 miles.
ASCENT	150 metres. Moderate.
START	Brynsiencyn public car park, Grid Ref 484671.
TO START	4 miles along the A4080 from the A5 in Llanfairpwll.

This links with Ride 13 and the proposed National Cycle Route. An off-road route from Llanidan to Plas Coch was tried but rejected as it was found to be too muddy in winter and only of footpath status rather than bridleway and thus not a right of way for cyclists. The lanes around Llanddaniel Fab are ideal for cycling and are excellent for views over the strait to the mountains of Snowdonia. There are some gentle downhill glides and very little traffic. Some of this route has been used for sponsored bike ride events. Should the ferry across the strait from the Mermaid be reinstated this would make an ideal way for cyclists to reach the mainland and the rest of the National Cycle Route.

THE RIDE

MAIN ROUTE 16 miles

The car park is opposite Y Groeslon pub by the layby and bus stop in Brynsiencyn. Turn sharp right into the narrow lane by the toilets. It is ½ mile gently downhill to the beautiful derelict church of St Nidan. Turn left and ride up the hill along a lovely old lane, lined with ancient lime and horse chestnuts, for ½ mile to the top. Emerge through stone gateposts, **with care**, onto the A4080 and go straight across into the narrow lane opposite. It is a slightly undulating 1½ miles to a small cross roads. Turn right signed Llanddaniel Fab and Bryn Celli Ddu.

(Or for a **Short Cut** (10 miles) omitting Llanddaniel turn left and rejoin Main Route instructions at *)

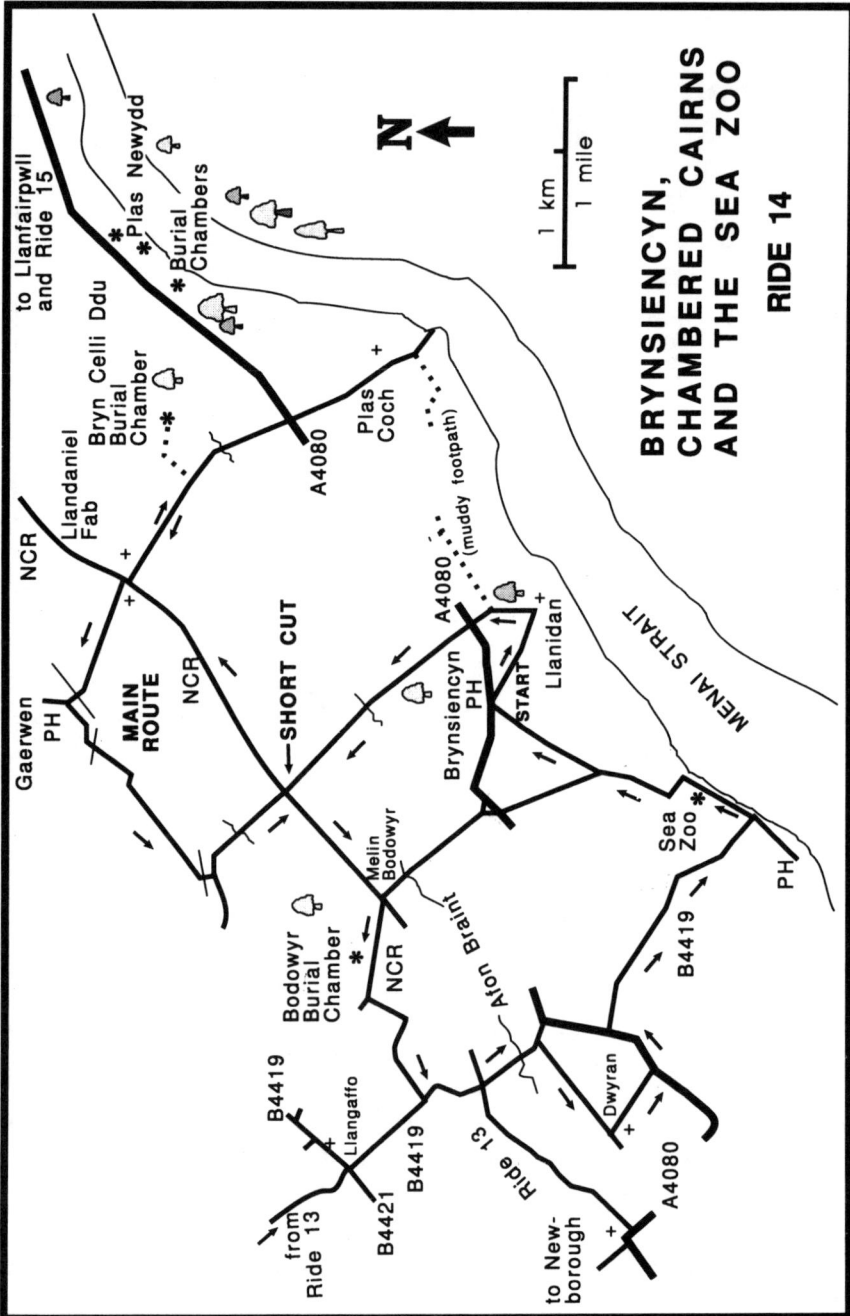

BRYNSIENCYN,
CHAMBERED CAIRNS
AND THE SEA ZOO

RIDE 14

N

1 km
1 mile

to Llanfairpwll
and Ride 15

Plas Newydd

* Burial Chambers

Bryn Celli Ddu
Burial Chamber

Llandaniel
Fab

Plas
Coch

A4080

A4080

(muddy footpath)

Llanidan

MENAI STRAIT

NCR

Gaerwen
PH

NCR

MAIN
ROUTE

SHORT CUT

Brynsiencyn
PH

START

Sea
Zoo

PH

Melin
Bodowyr

NCR

B4419

Bodowyr
Burial Chamber

Afon Braint

Dwyran

B4419

Llangaffo

Ride 13

A4080

B4419

B4421

from
Ride 13

to New-
borough

MAIN ROUTE continued...

Pass a golf driving range then at the outskirts of the village of **Llanddaniel Fab** pass a house, Y Berllan, on the left with a wonderful garden and huge duck pond just visible behind. Then pass a couple of chapels. In the village turn left (OR See **Detour**) at the T-junction opposite the old post office, then pass a shop (now closed).

DETOUR TO BRYN CELLI DDU 1 mile each way

Turn right at the village and glide down for ½ mile. At the bottom of a hill opposite Ysgol Parc y Bont a track on the left leads to the burial chamber. It is well worth a visit and is only ½ mile along the potholed track. (There is a small parking place here just past the school but do not block the entrance if you start here.) To return to the village climb back up the hill to Llanddaniel Fab and from this direction turn right and immediately left.

MAIN ROUTE continued...

On the next downhill section my record speed so far of 31 mph was reached! Go down to the level crossing—be prepared to brake! Pass the Dinam Arms and turn first left into a narrow lane. Cross a goods railway and continue for a mile along this pleasant winding lane to cross the main railway line and turn left at the T-junction. After ½ mile cross a stream and after another ½ mile turn right at the tiny cross roads where the * **Short cut** rejoins by the house Groeslon yr Odyn.

After ½ mile at another small cross roads by Melin Bodowyr turn right into a very narrow lane which has grass up the middle. It is uphill for ½ mile to reach Bodowyr. There is a gate on the right with a stile and information plaque. It is a few yards' stroll through the field to the burial chamber. Then continue for about a mile along the winding lane to the T-junction at the end. There are views to the right of a standing stone and the spire of Llangaffo church. Turn left onto a wider road (the B4419).

After ¼ mile go straight across a minor crossroads (this is the link with Ride 13). Cross the Afon Braint by Pont Mynach and then turn first right signed Dwyran (just before the main road). After ½ mile enter the village and turn first left by the post office. Ride through the village, passing the shop (open 7 days 7-9). Go down the hill to the main road by the Tal Ponciau bar and restaurant. (You could do a detour—right and left at the staggered cross roads—to visit a working farm, Fferm ar Waith.)

Turn left and follow the A4080 for ½ mile. Turn first right, **with care**, onto the B4419 signed Foel. It is 1½ miles mainly downhill; there is a post box near the end—be ready to stop or you will end up in the sea! There are splendid views over the strait to Caernarfon and the castle. To the right in the distance is the aerial which makes a good landmark for Ride 20.

A short detour to the right brings you to the remains of the old pier from which the Foel ferry used to cross the strait to Caernarfon. On the right is the Mermaid Inn and just before it the entrance to Fferm Foel/Farm Park. Turn left along the shore to the Sea Zoo. This road is narrow and can be busy on summer weekends with people coming to visit the zoo. Go left round the bend and gently uphill for a mile to Brynsiencyn. Pass the workshops and pottery. Y Groeslon pub is opposite on the left. Cross the road carefully and ride into the car park.

OTHER INFORMATION

SEA ZOO
This is a fascinating place and well worth a visit. In my opinion it is the best tourist attraction on the island and is good value as the ticket is an all day one ie you can leave and re-enter. It has an interesting collection of aquatic life from round the North Wales coast, an imitation shipwreck, a wave tank, touch pool, gift shop and snack bar. It is housed in the old lobster hatchery and has a display of the life of a lobster. It is open 7 days a week for most of the year from 10-5. Admission charge, tel 01248 430411.

WORKING FARMS
Foel Farm Park *off the A4080 has animals inside and outside, tractor rides, farm walks, rare breeds, home made ice cream, country cafe, gift shop and even sheep milking. It is open daily from Easter to October 10.30-5.30, tel 01248 430646.*

Bryntirion Working Farm *just off the A4080 at Dwyran (follow brown signs with a dragon symbol). It has antique farm machinery, game hatchery, milking display, fishing, organics, wood turning, tea room and exhibition, picnic and children's play area. Tours are at 11, 2, and 4. It is open from Whit till September, tel 01248 430232.*

BURIAL CHAMBERS
Bryn Celli Ddu *is one of the most famous chambered burial mounds. It dates from between 1500 and 2000BC. Inside were found flints, beads, skeletons and a stone with patterns—one of the earliest items of decoration in Britain. This stone is now in the museum in Cardiff.*

Bodowyr *dates from the Neolithic Period, 4000-2000BC, and was used for communal burials. The entrance passage was formerly to the east side. All of it was previously covered in a mound of earth but it has been excavated so the huge stones can be clearly seen. It is impressive and well worth the short walk through a field.*

Bryn yr Hen Bobl *'Hill of the Old People' is within the grounds of Plas Newydd. Inside were found human remains which showed grisly evidence of cannibalism.*

Bodowyr burial chamber

BRYNSIENCYN
This used to be a centre for worship by the Druids but nothing remains now of their once great temple at **Tre-Dryw**. *There are remains of a stone circle called* **Castell Bryngwyn** *at Grid Ref 465671. There is also a Romano-Celtic earthwork called* **Caer Leb** *at Grid Ref 473674. This has a pentagonal enclosure surrounded by banks and ditches.*

LLANIDAN
The old parish church of St Nidan is an interesting ruin. It is presently having some restoration work. Local legend has it that the stoup in the back porch never ran dry and that the water had healing qualities. It has a stone shield dated 1569 inside and old arches alongside.

LLANDDANIEL FAB
This also used to be a centre for Druidical worship. The natural world used to be held sacred and gods and goddesses gave their names to rivers such as the Afon Braint which was named after Brigantia. There is an attractive spired church at Llanedwen.

PLAS NEWYDD
This is a National Trust property open to the public from April to October from 12-5 every day except Saturdays, the grounds and shop open at 11. In October it is

open on Fridays and Sundays only. Last admission is 4.30, tel 01248 714795. It is the home of the Marquess of Anglesey. The mansion house was built in the 18th century of marble from Moelfre. Its most interesting contents include the famous Whistler mural and some Whistler cartoons. Short strolls are possible round the grounds which slope down to the strait. The Menai Centre and Nelson Centre, run by Cheshire Education for various arts, outdoor activities and fieldwork courses are also here. There is a cafe, toilets and NT shop which you can visit without paying to go in the mansion or grounds. These are always open on Friday and weekends from 11-5.

THE PUBS
The Mermaid Inn (Free House), overlooking the strait at Foel, serves bar snacks, coffee and meals and has a beer garden.
Y Groeslon in Brynsiencyn (Ansells) serves bar meals and has a children's menu.
Dinam Arms (Burtonwood) is at the edge of Gaerwen.

RIDE 15

MENAI BRIDGE TO LLANGEFNI
AND LLANFAIRPWLL

ROUTE Menai Bridge—Four Crosses—Penmynedd—Ceint—
Talwrn—Rhosmeirch—Llyn Cefni—Llangefni—
Ceint—Llanfairpwll—Menai Bridge

DISTANCE 21 miles/34 km. Or two loops: Menai Bridge to
Ceint, 12 miles; Ceint to Llyn Cefni, 9 miles.

ASCENT First loop, 180 metres. Second loop, 180 metres. Hilly.

START Menai Bridge car park, Grid Ref 558721. Or Llyn
Cefni car park, Grid Ref 452783. Or Llanfairpwll
station, Grid Ref 526716.

TO START A5 and A4080 to Menai Bridge (pay car park behind
Bulkeley Arms). Or, A5 and A5114 to Llangefni, then
B5110 and about 2 miles on the B5111 to Llyn Cefni
(car park just before the bottom of the hill on left).
Or, A5 and A4080 to Llanfairpwll (NB Pringle's car
park is private and chained when shop is closed).

Since the route goes against the 'grain' of the NW-SE ridges it is rather hilly. We cross the ridge between the Cefni and the Braint on the outward and return. Good views and good glides are the reward. There are lovely quiet lanes especially on the return. The three towns of Menai Bridge, Llangefni and Llanfairpwll have plenty of amenities. They are only small towns and normally not too bad to cycle through. Llangefni is busier on its market days of Thursday and Saturday. It is a convenient route for those coming by train or from over the bridge. It links with Rides 1 and 3 and to the projected NCR for those wanting longer routes. There is opportunity for a short off-road ride beside Llyn Cefni.

There is more main road (a mile between Llanfairpwll and Menai Bridge) on this ride than on any other. Due to the longer distance, the climbs, towns and main road this ride is less suitable for younger children than the rest of the routes. But I thoroughly recommend it for others as it is splendid!

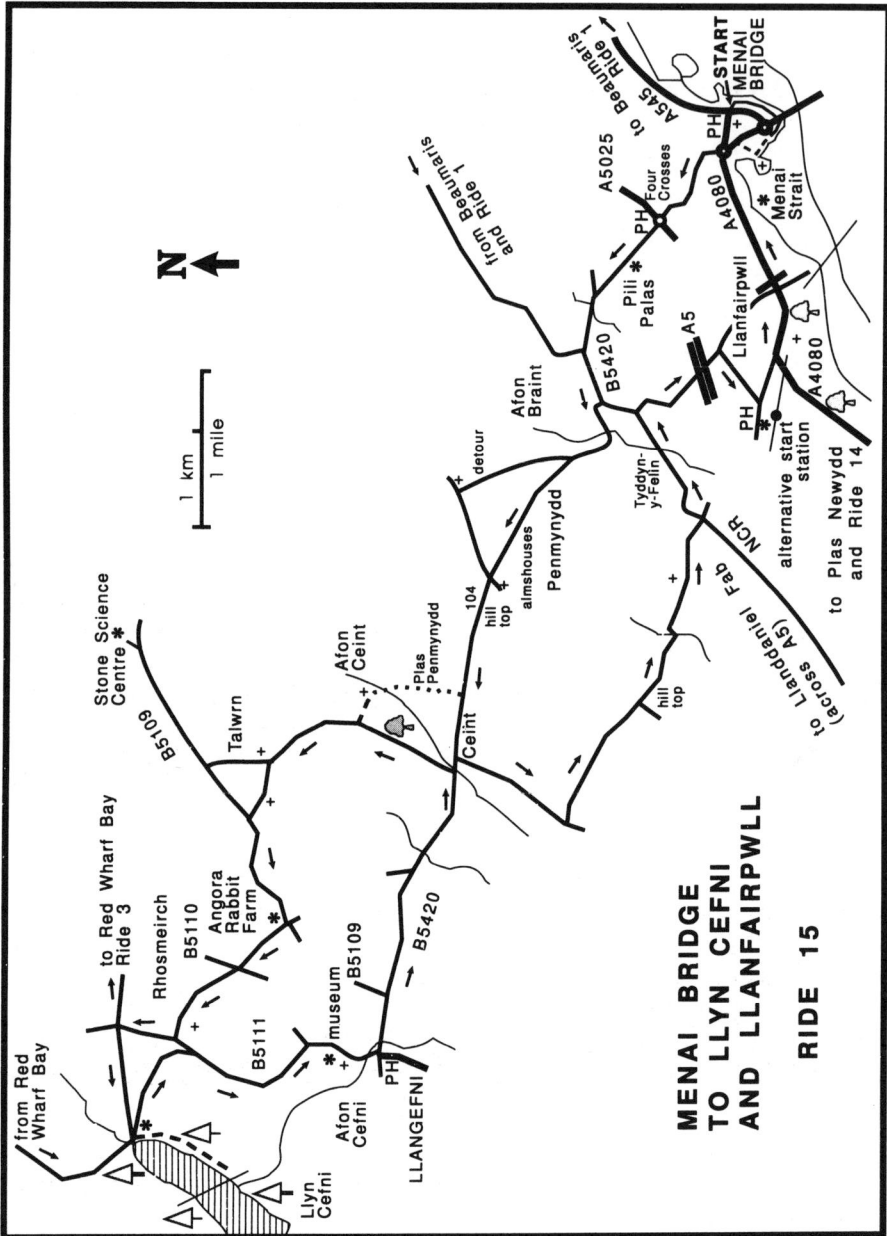

MENAI BRIDGE
TO LLYN CEFNI
AND LLANFAIRPWLL

RIDE 15

N

1 km
1 mile

START
MENAI
BRIDGE

to Beaumaris
A545

from Beaumaris
and Ride 1

PH

A5025

Four
Crosses

PH

Pili
Palas *

B5420

A5

A4080

Llanfairpwll

A4080

* Menai
Strait

PH

alternative start
station *

to Plas Newydd
and Ride 14

Afon
Braint

detour

Penmynydd

almshouses

104
hill
top

Tyddyn-
y-Felin

NCR
Fab 8

Llanddaniel Fab
(to across A5)

hill
top

Stone Science
Centre *

B5109

Afon
Ceint

Plas
Penmynydd

Talwrn

Ceint

Rhosmeirch

B5110

Angora Rabbit
Farm *

B5111

to Red Wharf Bay
Ride 3

B5109

museum *

B5420

PH

LLANGEFNI

Afon
Cefni

from Red
Wharf Bay

Llyn
Cefni

114

The route would be fine for children if you omit the main road, Menai Bridge and the Butterfly Farm as follows: take the lane through the middle of Llanfairpwll (see map) up to the safe bridge crossing over the A5, then after ½ mile turn right and in ¼ mile turn left onto the B5420 (at Grid Ref 527733) just before the Afon Braint.

For the less energetic you could make it two rides very easily as Ceint is the centre of a figure of 8 shape (see map).

THE RIDE

MAIN ROUTE 21 miles

The **recommended start** is the pay car park behind the Bulkeley Arms in **Menai Bridge**. There are plenty of shops and a fish and chip shop along the

Menai Bridge

main street. Ride along Dale Street opposite the pub to the roundabout by the Britannia garage and turn right, **with care**. The short cut omitting Menai Bridge joins here.

Follow the Amlwch sign and climb steeply uphill at first and then more gently, passing the old Menai Bridge reservoir (which is being looked after as a small nature reserve) and then the David Hughes school. At the roundabout go straight across, **with great care,** by the Four Crosses pub onto the B5420 signed Llangefni. This road is in common with Ride 1 for a mile but in the opposite direction.

Pass **Pili Palas** (Butterfly Farm) which has a cafe. It is over a mile along this undulating road. Cross the Afon Braint by an old farm, Sarn Fraint, the oldest part having a similar style to Lake District farms. At **Penmynydd** is a post office and garage selling ice creams and soft drinks etc. Pass the old almshouses: a line of low cottages on the left. The house called Carreg Sant holds the key to St Gredifael's church. This can be seen by detouring down a narrow lane to the right (see map).

Half way down the steep hill is a track on the right to Plas Penmynydd. Take **care** if you cross this road to go along the track to look at the outside of the house. Then return and ride down to the bottom of the hill to the tiny hamlet of **Ceint**.

For the **Menai Bridge Loop only,** the way back is to turn left just before the river and join the instructions at * below.

MAIN ROUTE continued...
Cross the Ceint and a disused railway track. Turn immediately right, **with care,** signed Talwrn. This is a beautiful narrow lane lined with old ash trees. Pass a track to Eglwys Llanffinan (the other end of the footpath past Plas Penmynydd). Continue straight on, passing two right turns. At the edge of the village of Talwrn turn first left along a narrow lane with a grassy middle. At the end turn left onto the B5109 for an undulating ¾ mile.

On a bend at the crossroads, turn right by the Angora Rabbit Farm. There is now a 4 ton weight restriction (heavy cyclists take note!). Go downhill for ½ mile and straight on at the crossroads with the B5110 onto another narrow lane. At the T-junction in the small village of Rhosmeirch turn right for the lake (or left and immediately left again onto the B5111 to omit it and go direct to Llangefni). Pass Rhosmeirch primary school. At the crossroads turn left and ride gently downhill on a lane which is in common with Ride 3. At the main road turn left and follow the B5111 for a few yards to turn first right, **with care,** to the picnic spot in the forest near **Llyn Cefni**. You are 11½ miles from Menai Bridge.

OFF-ROAD DETOUR 1 mile
You could ride ½ mile along the track with glimpses of the lake and then back to the picnic spot. From the hide you may see coot, swans and ducks.

MAIN ROUTE continued...
The picnic place here at Llyn Cefni makes a good **alternative start**. Turn

right, **with care**, onto the B5111, via the edge of Rhosmeirch for 1½ miles towards Llangefni. Pass Oriel Ynys Mon on the left. Turn right at the end, **with care**, and follow the one way system into the town of Llangefni.

In **Llangefni** town centre pass the post office and shops. Turn left at the clocktower passing more shops and a fish and chip shop (or if you want other amenities turn right first before continuing). Follow the B5109 signed Pentraeth which becomes the B5420. Climb away from the town and go straight on signed Penmynydd. There is a derelict windmill on the hill to the left. Pass a church and the Coleg Menai. It is gently downhill to cross a tributary of the Cefni. The road is then undulating with hazel hedges. Pass the Talwrn sign, cross a bridge and turn right, **with care**, in the hamlet of **Ceint**, onto a minor road. * **Menai Bridge Loop only rejoins here.**

Climb gently for a mile or so. Turn first left along a narrow lane which is grassy in the middle. Climb more steeply passing a delightful wooded valley on the right. At the house Fron Isaf you are nearly at the top and the view opens towards the mainland. Pass a right turn and by the entrance to Cefn Du you have reached the summit. There are superb views to the mountains of Snowdonia.

It is a pleasant downhill run from here. The lane has a mixture of hedges and earth covered banks, excellent for wild flowers in spring. Pass the chapel Pencarneddi, with dates of 1786 and 1928, and follow the winding lane down past several farms. At the end of the lane turn left at the T-junction and continue straight on for ¾ mile, passing an old churn bench and crossing the line of huge pylons. It is gently down along this narrow lane to cross a tiny stream, then start to climb and near the top turn right, signed Llanfairpwll. The lane winds downhill, eventually widening to cross the bypass by a bridge to reach the outskirts of Llanfairpwll. At the T-junction turn right and pass bungalows, terraced houses, a shop, bakery and a Welsh Presbyterian Chapel.

At the main road in **Llanfairpwll** turn right, **with care**, opposite the Ty Gwyn Hotel to visit the station (**alternative start**). A few yards down the road on the left is a huge car park for the information office and James Pringle shop. There are many tourist orientated shops here.

From the station turn right, **with care**, onto the main road, passing Ty Gwyn Hotel and the shops, take-away and toilets. Go straight on. The road becomes the A4080 to Menai Bridge. The road is fairly busy but it does have a pavement for most of its length. It would be safer if younger children were allowed to use it. Look out for the Women's Institute and the Llanfair Gate toll house and go straight on.

Pass the Marquess of Anglesey's Column. Go under the A5 and be careful of traffic coming off the Britannia Bridge and turning across this road. Go downhill passing laybys on the right with superb views of Telford's suspension bridge, Church Island and the strait. A good place for photos! The pavement is better on the offside. It is just over a mile to the roundabout by the Britannia Garage. (For a Short Cut omitting Menai Bridge turn left here.)

Go straight across, **with care**, into Dale Street/Lon Cylbedlam. Pass the Catholic church, bakery and Chinese take-away. At Uxbridge Square go straight across, **with care**, by the Bulkeley Arms into Water Street/Stryd y Paced to visit the Auckland Arms or Liverpool Arms or see the slipway at Porth y Wrach. If you turn left in front of the Liverpool Arms you will come to the entrance to the short drive leading to the pier. Then return to the square.

OTHER INFORMATION

LLANFAIRPWLL
is short for Llanfairpwllgwyngyllgogerychwyrndrobwllllantysiliogogogoch, or St Mary's Church in the hollow of white hazel near a rapid whirlpool and the church of St Tysilio by the red cave. The name is probably a Victorian invention to attract the tourists—which it still does! You can buy a platform ticket with the name—the

The station

longest in Britain. The main **Tourist Information Office** for the island (tel 01248 713177) is just inside Pringle's shop (tel 01248 717171) next to the station. It also has a cafe and two narrow gauge steam locomotives as well as knitwear, crafts, souvenirs and railway memorabilia. The Women's Institute by Llanfair Gate was the first in Britain, having been founded in 1915.

The toll house at Llanfair Gate displays the toll prices but it predates the bicycle of course! The A5 was Britain's last toll road and was freed from charges in 1895. The A5 was completed in 1826. It was designed by Thomas Telford and carried mail coaches from London. Steamships from Holyhead then completed the journey to Ireland. When the Menai suspension bridge was opened coaches could travel the 460 km/286 miles to London in 27 hours. In 1850 the railway was finished and the journey from London to Holyhead was reduced to 9½ hours.

Marquess Of Anglesey's Column As this is 90 feet high and stands on a mound 25 feet above sea level, not surprisingly it commands stupendous views but you have to climb about 115 steps to get to the top. I may have lost count and not being too happy with precipitous drops I'm not recommending it to the faint hearted! It is made of marble from Moelfre and was built to commemorate William Paget who lost his leg fighting with Wellington at the Battle of Waterloo and was made the first Marquess of Anglesey. He was the first person ever to have a jointed artificial leg!

PENMYNYDD
This quiet rural village is steeped in history. The tiny almshouses were built in 1620 and were originally 10 houses! They were converted into 5 houses in the 1960s.

Plas Penmynydd was the home of the Tudors for 300 years. Owain Tudor, who was the grandfather of Henry VII was born and lived here until going to London to join the army of Henry V. He was successful and became part of the court circle. When Henry V died Owain secretly married Henry's widow Catherine, and was later hanged for this at the Tower of London. The present house dates from the 16th century. It became derelict, was bought privately and renovated. It is now a private dwelling and not open to the public but a public footpath does pass in front of it. The present church of **St Gredifael** dates from the 14th century but there has been a church on the site since the 6th century. There is an elaborate alabaster tomb inside the church of Gronw Tudor and his wife Myfanwy. Gronw was an uncle of Owain and a friend of Edward the Black Prince.

A folk legend from Penmynydd about a serpent reminds us that adders are common on the island and that one shouldn't kick them when dead or alive! The 'serpent of Penhesgyn' saw its own reflection in a pool. It attacked itself and died. The son of the household kicked it and was stung with the venom still present. He died,

Plas Penmynydd

bringing home a prophecy of a curse on the household.

LLANGEFNI

Llangefni is the county town and has a busy open air market on Thursday and Saturday. It has a sports centre with a swimming pool. There is a pleasant short walk along a stretch of the River Cefni valley called the Dingle.

Oriel Ynys Mon is on the B5111. The history of the island from prehistoric times to the present and its ecology are presented in imaginative modern displays. It houses a major exhibition of the wonderful wildlife paintings of C.F. Tunnicliffe as well as visiting exhibitions and is well worth a visit. It has a gift shop and cafe. It is open from 10.30-5 on Tuesday to Sunday and Bank Holiday Mondays. Entrance charge, tel 01248 724444.

TALWRN

The Stone Science Centre is a mainly personal collection of minerals, fossils and semi-precious stone jewellery. It also has a fossil dinosaur bone and fragments of a dinosaur shell and gastroliths. Some specimens are for sale. There is a picnic area and also pet goats. It is open daily from Easter to October and has a small charge. From Talwrn carry on through the village (instead of turning left) then turn right

120

onto the B5109 and it is 1 mile along the road on the left at an old rectory, Bryn Eglwys, Llanddyfan.

The Angora Rabbit Farm is a charming place where you can see the rabbits and learn about rabbit care and wool preparation. Woolly jumpers are for sale! It is at Slieve Donard, Talwrn Road, Llangefni, tel 01248 750297 and is open from 10-4 all year and has a small charge.

Menai Bridge and Pili Palas see Ride 1.
Llyn Cefni see Ride 3

THE PUBS
The Liverpool Arms (Greenalls) is in Menai Bridge and does good home made-food. The Bulkeley Arms (Robinsons), Auckland Arms (Greenalls) are also in Menai Bridge and serve bar food. There are several cafes too.
The Ty Gwyn Hotel (Youngers) and Penrhos Arms (Greenalls) are in Llanfairpwll and serve food.
Several in Llangefni.

BANGOR TO GLASINFRYN AND BETHESDA RIDE 16

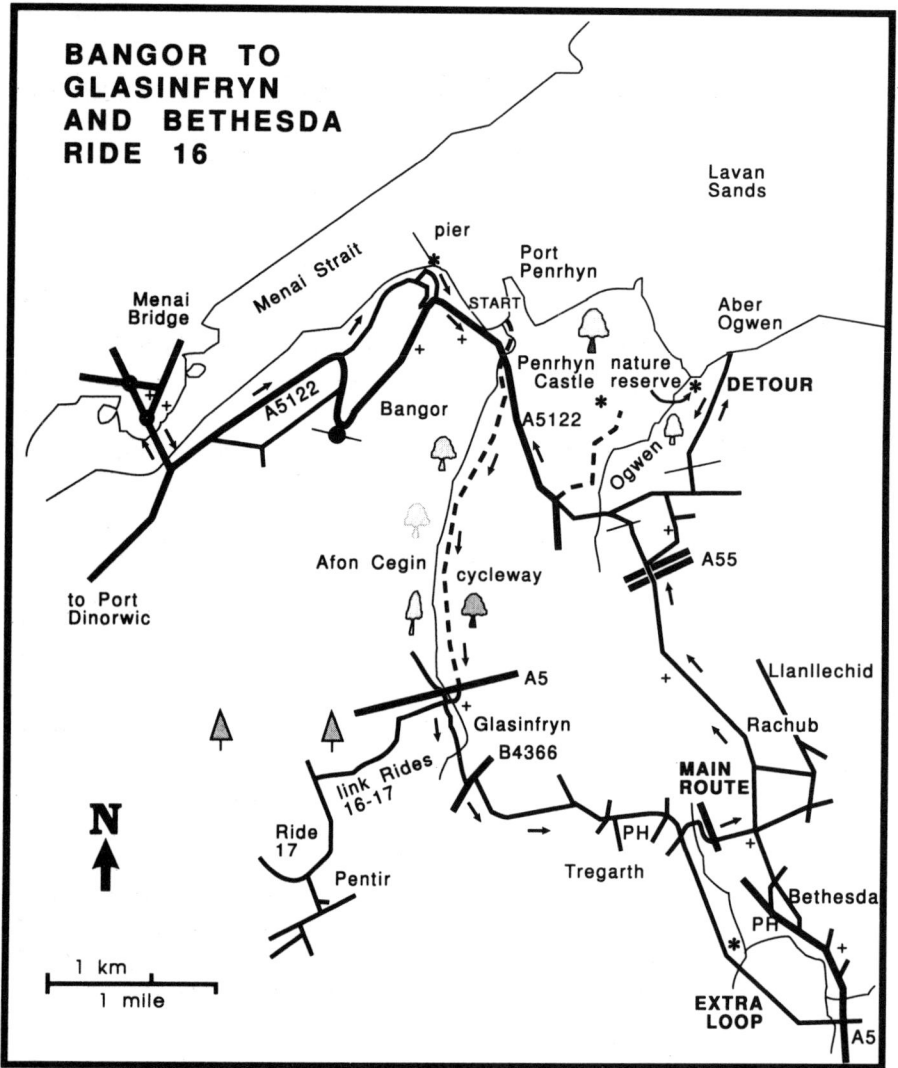

Lavan Sands

pier

Port Penrhyn

START

Aber Ogwen

Menai Bridge

Menai Strait

Penrhyn Castle

nature reserve

DETOUR

A5122

A5122

Bangor

Ogwen

to Port Dinorwic

A55

Afon Cegin

cycleway

Llanllechid

A5

Rachub

Glasinfryn
B4366

link Rides 16-17

MAIN ROUTE

N

Ride 17

PH

Tregarth

Pentir

Bethesda

PH

1 km

1 mile

EXTRA LOOP

A5

BANGOR TO GLASINFRYN AND BETHESDA

ROUTE   Menai Bridge link to Bangor—Port Penrhyn to
Glasinfryn via cycleway—road return route:
Tregarth—Bethesda—Rachub—Llanllechid—Tal y
Bont—Aber Ogwen—Llandegai—Bangor

DISTANCE   10 miles/16 km + Menai link, 2½ miles each way,
Aber Ogwen, 3 miles and Bethesda loop, 3 miles.
Cycleway only, 6 miles return.

ASCENT   Cycleway 70 metres, very gentle. Main Route via
Aber Ogwen 220 metres. Quite a lot!

START   Port Penrhyn, Grid Ref 5593727, or Bangor Station, or
Bangor Pier, or Menai Bridge.

TO START   A5 or A55 to Bangor. A4087 from station, then A5122
briefly, turn left on bend down to Port Penrhyn
(signed Toc H and Port).

With young children the Bangor to Glasinfryn cycleway is a good
introduction to cycling. If you parked at the start of the cycleway at Port
Penrhyn and avoided any roads it would be a safe route just doing the
cycleway there and back. This would only be **3 miles each way** and should
be OK even for the youngest members of the family. The Road Return
Route adds interest and length and a few hills for the more experienced
cyclists! Parking by Bangor Pier or Port Penrhyn is preferable.

THE RIDE

LINK FROM MENAI BRIDGE ½ miles each way
From Menai Bridge, cross the Telford suspension bridge. At the end is the
Antelope pub. Turn left, **with care**, at the roundabout to Bangor on the A5.
After a mile turn left down Siliwen Road. It is residential at first then
narrow, winding and wooded. There are good views over the straits and a
modern stone circle. The traffic lights, where there has been road
subsidence, might not detect cyclists, so wave at them!

Sweep down to the left to visit Bangor Pier. There is a small **car park** here.

Continue along Garth Road. There are several pubs, Y Garth, the Ship Launch and the Union. The first shop sells ice creams and soft drinks and the second sells pottery. Pass Dickie's boatyard and turn left onto the main road by the old British School dating from 1848.

LINK FROM BANGOR STATION

If starting at the **railway station** cross the road with care and ride down the A5122 to Dickie's boatyard where the link to Menai Bridge joins. Ride with care along Ffordd Traeth/Beach Road, passing Hirael Bay restaurant, a fish and chip shop and the Nelson pub. The shore often has shelduck feeding and a wreck buried in the sand is just visible. Leaving Bangor cycle **with care** up the main road the A5122. (There is a wide pavement and it would be safer if children were allowed to use this.) Either go down the road on the left to **Port Penrhyn** to the recommended start, or keep on the main road, pass the YHA on the right and take the next right turning for Maesgeirchen housing estates on Penrhyn Avenue. Cross the road **with care**. Immediately on the left of this road is the bike and pedestrian stile leading to the **cycleway**. It is not signed at present. The only sign is the tiny gas pipeline crossing marker! The narrow cyclepath crosses the bridge parallel to the main road over the Afon Cegin. Turn right onto the much wider track and follow the Main Route.

MAIN ROUTE FROM PORT PENRHYN 10 miles

From Bangor turn left off the main road, pass TOC H on the left and a private entrance to Penrhyn on the right. Take the middle track and cross the river by the lower of the two bridges down to the boat yard and **car park**. The cycleway starts here and follows the line of a disused railway. It crosses the river by a new bridge.

The cycleway is easy to ride on and follows the beautiful Afon Cegin. It is mainly through mixed deciduous woodland. There is new gravel on the track and yellow painted boulders to stop cars by access points to some roads. There is access via a footbridge to the back of the Maesgeirchen estate to the right and on the left to an industrial estate so it serves the needs of local people well. The track goes through an arch of the impressive sandstone bridge carrying the main line railway. There is another tiny bridge for the lane which goes to Llandegai. The views are more open now with glimpses of the mountains ahead across the sheep pastures. There is a steady but gentle climb.

Keep on the upper narrow path to a stile gate. The huge pylons cross overhead here at the end of the track. Decide whether to return the same way via the cycleway or to do the Road Return Route.

Ghost train

MAIN ROUTE (RETURNING BY ROAD) 7 miles

Emerge onto the road and turn left. Go under the bridge which carries the Bangor bypass. Turn first left for **Glasinfryn**, a village with several chapels but no longer shop nor pub. Pass the Chapel Bethmaaca, then a derelict one whose 'Lease of Site was granted by Lord Penrhyn 1892' and the next chapel which is still used. Cross the Afon Cegin and pass the post office. At the T-junction turn left and immediately right, **with care**, onto the B4409 signed Tregarth. Beside the tiny stream is the old mill house Tyddyn Felin and then Felin Hen cottage with ducks and hens. The continuation of the disused railway is inaccessible and impenetrable at present, but there are plans to extend the cycleway to Bethesda. Continue on the road with pleasant views of the hills.

Climb gently uphill to **Tregarth**. Pass the church Eglwys y Santes Fair, a cemetery surrounded by yews, Shiloh Church, the road to Sling on the right, to Mynedd Llandegai and then the one to Dob. Go uphill panting hard past Pant yr Ardd! Then pass a telephone, and the tiny Tregarth post office.

There are splendid views of the mountains from Tregarth. Take the fourth turning on the left signed A5 just outside Tregarth by a phone box for the **Main Route** or keep straight on for the **Bethesda Extra Loop.**

MAIN ROUTE continued...

Turn left at the phone box and go steeply downhill to the River Ogwen. There is a slate milestone set in the stone bridge on the right and access to the river through the wall on the left (NB the river is fast and deep here and not suitable for paddling). Cross the disused railway again and at the crossroads go straight across the A5, **with care**, signed Rachub. It is quite a climb but is only for ½ mile. The superb views of the mountains compensate for the hard work! At the top is a bench if you need a rest! At this minor cross roads turn left into a narrow lane. The Extra Loop rejoins here.

EXTRA LOOP 3 miles

Continue straight on up the hill. Pass the new industrial estate, Coed y Parc and the entrance to the Penrhyn Slate Quarries. Cross the river and pass a paint works. There are old slate dumps here and the entrance to the Joys of Life Country Park. Turn left onto the A5 and cycle into **Bethesda**. Pass the Church of Jerusalem and a couple of chapels and a supermarket. There are plenty of food and drink outlets, eg fish and chip shop, Chinese takeaway, and the Bull, Pant y Brennin, and Victoria pubs.

Turn right, **with care**, signed the library, police and free car park. Cycle steeply uphill and bend left. Pass Ysgol Dyffryn Ogwen. At the staggered junction turn right and left into Ffordd Coetmor. It is now a pleasanter lane. Pass a chapel surrounded by pine and yew. Go straight on at the tiny cross road to rejoin the Main Route.

MAIN ROUTE continued...

There is now a 2 mile run mainly downhill as a relief from all the climbing! Some of the descent is steep so check brakes first! There are plenty of wild flowers including stitchwort and bluebells. The views of Anglesey and Penrhyn Castle are excellent. Pass the entrance to Cochwillan Old Hall (viewing by appointment) on the left between the pylons. At the T-junction turn left (signed Llanllechid and Bethesda to the right) on a wide bend. Cross the new road by a bridge and turn immediately right, **with care**. Follow the narrow winding lane past Eglwys St Cross. Turn left onto the old A5 to return to **Bangor** or...

DETOUR TO ABER OGWEN AND NATURE RESERVE 3 miles

Turn right onto old A5, now declassified, and immediately left. It is a mile gently downhill to the sea, passing the walled wooded grounds of Penrhyn

Castle to your left. The Spinnies Bird Hide is on the left. You can leave bikes secured to walk to it. There is a small car park at the end overlooking the Lavan sands with excellent views across the strait to Beaumaris. There is a footpath along the shore towards Llanfairfechan. It makes an ideal picnic place. There are plenty of waders, ducks and often swans to watch. It is of course 1 mile back uphill to the old A5, passing some wild ramsons in the damper hedgebanks. Cross the railway and turn right, **with care**.

MAIN ROUTE continued...

After ½ mile gently uphill cross the River Ogwen at Llandegai. Turn right, **with care**, onto the A5122 by the entrance to **Penrhyn Castle**. It is about a mile slightly uphill to cross the Afon Cegin. Pass the YHA entrance whose lodge shows Cerberus, the three-headed dog, and a Welsh inscription. Turn next right off the main road and return to the start at **Port Penrhyn**.

Or continue on into Bangor for the station. Or to return to Menai Bridge turn right, **with care**, by Dickie's boatyard and retrace your outward route along Garth and Siliwen Roads.

OTHER INFORMATION

BANGOR

Bangor Pier *has several attractions, a maritime centre, toilets, cafe, bar and restaurant 10am-10pm, tel 01248 362807, small charge for adults on pier, no cycling. The Wheelhouse from the Norwegian flagship SS Asmund, built in 1900 and wrecked off Anglesey in 1930, is here. The centre was opened by Aled Eames, maritime historian, in 1991 The pier was reopened by the Marquess of Anglesey in 1988 after renovation.*

The Museum and Art Gallery *is found on Ffordd Gwynedd just behind the Post Office on Deiniol Road. It is open from Tuesday to Friday from 12.30-4.30 and Saturday from 10.30-4.30. Admission is free. It has a collection mainly relating to North Wales's history. There is a gift shop, tel 01248 353368.*

CYCLEWAY

The cycleway was constructed by Arfon council and is a delightful route through mixed deciduous woodland. The many trees include elder, hazel, sessile oak, sycamore, groups of poplars, elder, occasional elms, birch, hawthorn, blackthorn, horse chestnut, holly and Douglas fir. The ash and beech are mainly regenerating from cut stumps. Flowers include bluebells, herb robert, hedge woundwort, roses, honeysuckle, dogs mercury, wood anemone and spurge. In the damp hollows are woodrush, ferns, creeping jenny, flag iris, king cup, and arum lily. Birds seen include jay, chaffinch, robins, blackbirds in plenty and one buzzard. Speckled Wood butterflies abound and brilliant blue dragonflies dart over the river at the right time of year.

BETHESDA

The Joys of Life Country Park *was formerly Bryn Derwyn, the home farm of the manager of the Penrhyn quarry. It was converted in 1983 to a small museum concentrating on some of the original farm equipment and hobbies, especially model trains. There is a garden, pet ducks, nature trail, lake, bird hide, miniature railway, model village, refreshment room and craft shop. It is open from Easter to second Sunday in September on Tuesday to Sunday from 11-5 and Bank holiday Mondays. There is an entry charge, tel 01248 602122.*

PORT PENRHYN

This is the port from which slate from the Penrhyn quarries was shipped. It is now a small commercial port with a boat yard. Fresh fish is sold here.

PENRHYN CASTLE

This is a large mansion built as a neo-Norman castle by the owners of the slate quarries and is presently owned by the NT. It has a remarkable slate staircase, doll collection and steam engines. It is open from April to October daily except for Tuesdays. The castle itself is open from 12-5, 11-5 in July and August. Last Admission is 4.30. The grounds are open from 11-6. The park is very beautiful with woodland and a Victorian walled garden. There is an entry charge.

THE PUBS

The Antelope (Greenalls) is by the bridge, serves food and has a beer garden. Pubs in Bangor include:

Y Garth (Ansells) serves food from 12-2 and 7-9.

Ship Launch (Bass) serves food from 12-2.30

The Union (Burtonwood) serves morning coffee and hot and cold bar food from 12-2 and 6-8. Small beer garden overlooking marina.

The Nelson (Ansells).

Pant yr Ardd (Robinsons) is in Tregarth.

PORT DINORWIC (Y FELINHELI) TO PENTIR

ROUTE	Port Dinorwic—Crug Farm—Pont Rug (link to Ride 18)—Dinas Dinorwig—Pentir—Port Dinorwic—link to Menai Bridge and Anglesey.
DISTANCE	12 miles/19 km. Menai Link, 2½ miles each way. Caernarfon Link, 3 miles each way.
ASCENT	230 metres. A steep ascent from sea level at Port Dinorwic at the start, eventually reaches 160 metres.
START	Port Dinorwic (Y Felinheli). Public car park beside the sea, Grid Ref 523676.
TO START	A487 from Menai Bridge or Caernarfon or A4087 from Bangor. At the bypass roundabout, follow signs for Y Felinheli and then for the beach.

The lanes we use behind Port Dinorwic are wonderful for cycling: they are very quiet and through a pleasant rural landscape with extensive views both over the strait and to the mountains. The pretty village of Pentir makes a suitable destination with a choice of pub or cafe—both good.

The only drawback to the route is that there is quite a steep pull up from Port Dinorwic initially—this bit could even be walked! I feel it is better to have a short sharp climb at the beginning and good views and plenty of more gentle downhill later in the route. It also seems safer this way. The route is fairly short so it shouldn't be too strenuous and it allows for extra miles for those cycling from Anglesey or from Bangor or via a short section of cycleway from Caernarfon.

For those wanting a longer ride it links via Pont Rug with Ride 18. Also from Pentir one could cycle via Caerhun to Glasinfryn and so link with the cycleway to Port Penrhyn and hence Bangor for an alternative route. There are some bridleways in this area but I haven't included them as they are muddy and there is no need to avoid roads when they are as free from traffic and as pleasant as these.

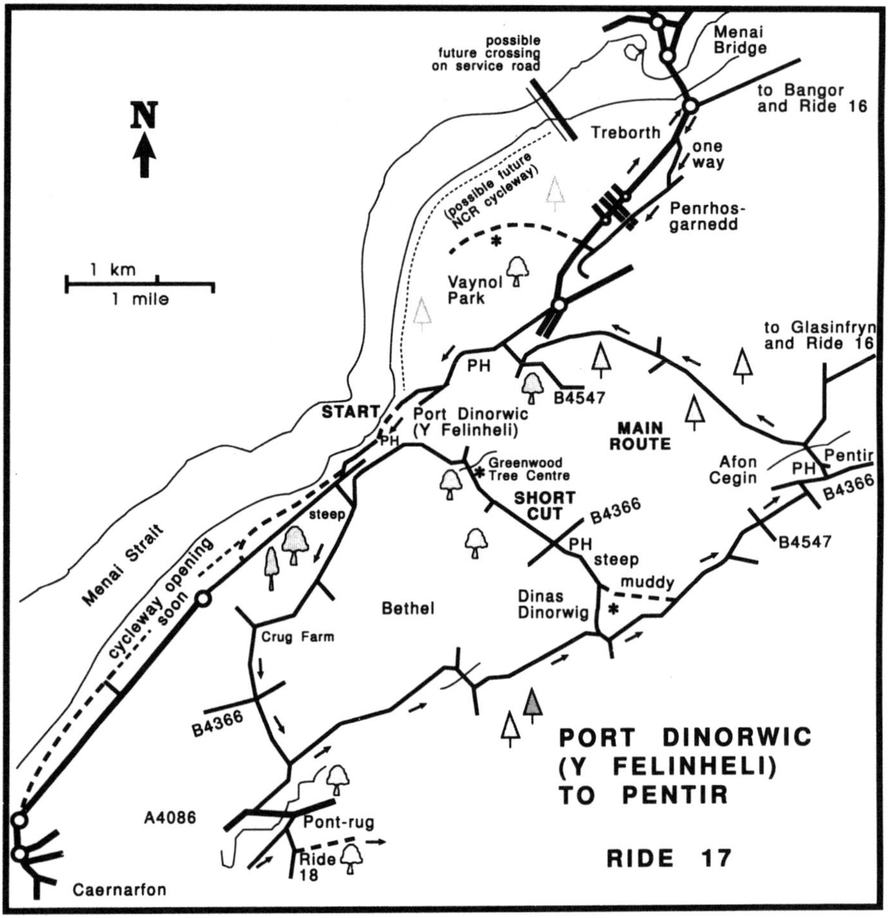

N

1 km
1 mile

possible
future crossing
on service road

Menai
Bridge

to Bangor
and Ride 16

Treborth

one
way

(possible future
NCR cycleway)

Penrhos-
garnedd

Vaynol
Park

to Glasinfryn
and Ride 16

PH

B4547

MAIN
ROUTE

START

Port Dinorwic
(Y Felinheli)

PH

Afon
Cegin

Pentir

PH

Greenwood
Tree Centre

B4366

SHORT
CUT

B4366

B4366

PH

steep

B4547

steep

Menai Strait

cycleway opening
soon

Bethel

Dinas
Dinorwig

muddy

Crug Farm

B4366

PORT DINORWIC
(Y FELINHELI)
TO PENTIR

A4086

Pont-rug

Ride
18

RIDE 17

Caernarfon

130

THE RIDE

LINK FROM MENAI BRIDGE 2½ miles each way

Cross the straits by the Telford suspension bridge. Turn right, **with care**, at the roundabout by the Antelope pub. Cycle uphill and turn first left into a narrow road, Ffordd Ty'n Clwt, prohibited to large vehicles and with a width restriction. Continue uphill and turn right at the T-junction onto a wider road, pass two chapels and a residential area. At the end of the houses cross the main pylon line and go over the new road. Bear right and then at the T-junction turn left.

There is a pavement and it would be safer if children were allowed to use it. It is a fast downhill glide to the roundabout at the bottom of the hill. It might be safer to dismount and cross the road before the roundabout and safer if one could use the pavement on the right alongside the high wall of the Vaynol estate as far as the bus stop before crossing to the correct side.

Pass a telephone, a bridge, the Ty Hanner Ffordd and then turn right, **with care**, over humps and downhill alongside the river. There are plenty of yachts to admire in the safe anchorage behind the lock gates. Pass the Tradewinds Restaurant. The next few yards are off-road. Follow the potholed track keeping to the landward side unless you want to take a look at the old harbour first and go across to the brown gate. Go through the derelict footpath stile and turn right onto the seafront past the toilets and Garddfon Inn onto Beach Road/Glan y Môr.

MAIN ROUTE 12 miles

There is a car park by the sea on Beach Road on the front at **Port Dinorwic**. The benches by the strait make an ideal picnic place with good views to Moel y don on Anglesey. Ride along to the boatyard and workshops and then prepare for 'the climb'! It is steeply uphill but only for a short distance. Pass the stile entrance to the cycleway labelled **Lôn Las Arfon** on the right just before the top. This is the **link from Caernarfon** and follows a disused railway. (There is a small car park on the left.)

At the top turn right at the T-junction, **with care**, onto the main road. Pass the chapel and turn first left uphill again. It soon becomes a quiet narrow lane and more importantly it levels off! The splendid views start here. Continue straight on past a left turning to Bethel. At the T-junction by Crug Farm turn left. This is a plant nursery and is worth a visit especially on the annual National Garden Scheme open day when the private garden is also open. This road is somewhat busier. Cross the B road by a slightly staggered cross roads. The next ½ mile is undulating. On the bend by the old converted Nazareth Chapel turn left to continue the ride, or go straight on to link with Ride 18.

Family cycling

LINK TO RIDE 18

Continue for ¼ mile, turn left onto the A4086, cross the lovely Afon Seiont by Pont Rug and turn first right, **with care**, to link with the Caernarfon Castle to Bryn Bras Castle Ride—see Map.

MAIN ROUTE continued...

From the old Nazareth Chapel there is a beautiful lane for 1½ miles. The old stone walls are covered with earth, forming banks reminiscent of those in Cornwall. They have abundant wild flowers best seen in spring or summer. There are now good views of Snowdon. Turn right at the T-junction and first left onto a very narrow lane. It is marked as a white track on the OS 1:50 000 map but incorrectly as a brown road on the 1:25 000 one. It is ideal for cyclists but is too narrow in parts for anything much wider! Follow it for a mile passing isolated farmsteads eg Cae Metta. You can see Pen Dinas ahead; it has a small copse of old pine trees but is mainly bracken clad.

At the T-junction at the end turn right, briefly steeply downhill and immediately first left onto another narrow lane. This climbs up for less than ¼ mile to the highest point on the ride, at 160 metres, near the top of Pen Dinas at 169 metres, at 6 miles from Port Dinorwic. The remains of Dinas Dinorwig are presumably hidden by the scrub on the private land. There are views of a young pine forest to the right, we once tried to walk on the path through it but it is a quagmire!

This lane is also good for flower spotting: there are yarrow, campion, harebell, self-heal, hawkweed, woodsage, stitchwort, hardheads, herb robert, sloe, rose, hogweed, foxglove etc as well as elder, oak and gorse. It is now more or less downhill all the way back. At first it is fairly steeply down and then more gently so. The views ahead to Penmaenmawr soon open up. (By gates on the left is a bridleway up and round the northern slopes of Pen Dinas, well used by horses but difficult for cycling, although it could make an alternative steep short cut back.)

Continue straight on ignoring a right fork, and at the bottom cross a B road by a telephone. Continue to the end of this lane. At the T-junction turn left and immediately right, **with care**, onto the main road. Turn first left into the village of **Pentir**. The pub is on the left and the Rainbow Court cafe on the right.

Follow the minor road down through the village, over the bridge across the Afon Cegin and turn immediately left by the Pont Felin sign. This is a pleasant lane for over a mile. It goes through a pine wood and past a huge substation, a major junction for the pylons from Wylfa on their way to the grid. After the wood at the end turn right and immediately left at a grassy triangle. Pass Hafod Uchaf and continue downhill. It is a splendid glide for a mile. The lane is grassy in the middle at first and later becomes a little steeper and is called Ffordd Fodolydd. Go under the new bypass and turn right, **with care**, onto the B4547. Arrive at the T-junction with the former A road.

RETURN LINK TO MENAI BRIDGE

Turn right, **with care**, onto the main road. Again it would be safer if one were allowed to use the pavement to the roundabout to turn left and safer to cross the road and use the pavement on the offside for the climb back up the hill. The entrance to Vaynol Park is part way up the hill via a gate in the big wall on the left. Follow the signs back to Menai Bridge. There is quite a lot of traffic and several newish roundabouts but there is a pavement for most of the way. The minor road used outward can't be used for the return as it is one way. (There is an off-road track via Treborth School, riding stables and University playing fields and Botanic Gardens road but it may well not be a public right of way.)

MAIN ROUTE continued...

Turn left onto the former A road and it is a mile back to Port Dinorwic. Turn right into the bumpy lane and cycle down by the river as described on Menai Bridge Link outward route.

OTHER INFORMATION

PORT DINORWIC/Y FELINHELI

It seems to have been decided that the name Port Dinorwic doesn't exist any more causing some confusion as it has been known as such by both Welsh and English speakers for a long time. Most of the other place name signs are rightly bilingual. Y Felinheli means 'the saltwater mill'. The new Port Dinorwic bypass isn't marked on the OS maps yet. This ride crosses the bypass safely by one bridge over and one under. The old A487 through Port Dinorwic village is now a quieter road and safer for cyclists since the bypass takes the fast through traffic.

There are plenty of amenities at the port and an attractive marina development centred around the river and the old harbour. The Seahorse and the Sail Loft Restaurants are on the front. The ride passes the site of the ancient hill fort of Dinas Dinorwig on the hill Pen Dinas. This is the highest point on the ride. Unfortunately it is on private land but the wild flowers of the banks and hedgerows are a delight here and the views are great.

LÔN LAS CYCLEWAY

The new cycleway and pedestrian path, opened on 15 September 1994, is on a disused railway line and starts beside the new Safeway Garage in Caernarfon. It is being extended into the town. It goes as far as Waterloo Dock Road and is bare of vegetation as yet. The next section is due to open in Spring 1995. At the Port Dinorwic end it starts near the top of the steep hill and goes as far as a bus stop on the main road. It is very pleasant and wooded.

PENTIR

Rainbow Court Cafe/Llys yr Enfys. Summer opening hours are 9.30-5 Monday to

Saturday for coffee shop, 6.30-8.30 every day except Tuesday and Sunday for restaurant, Sunday 4.30 for tea and late lunch. It has vegetarian alternatives.

GREENWOOD TREE CENTRE

This has forest walks in 17 acres of grounds. There is an all-weather visitor centre with exhibitions all about the world of trees. It also has a tea room and gift shop. It is found near Bethel off the B4366 one mile from the Gors Bach pub on the Short Cut (NB steep lanes over Pen Dinas) or can be reached from Part Dinorwic. It is open from Easter to September from 10-5.30 daily and less often at other times. Admission charge, tel 01248 671493.

VAYNOL PARK/GLAN FAENOL

This is a National Trust property on the link to Menai Bridge. There are country walks, picnic sites, woodland and parkland. It is open from dawn to dusk. One can cycle for a mile from the entrance as far as a car park and then explore on foot. It is hoped that the National Cycle Route may soon link up through here to avoid the roads.

THE PUBS

The Antelope (Greenalls) on link to Menai Bridge, has a restaurant and a beer garden.

Ty Hanner Ffordd (Ansells) at the edge of Port Dinorwic serves bar food and families are welcome.

The Tradewinds (Greenalls) by the marina restaurant and bar snacks, children welcome.

Garddfon Inn (Burtonwood) Beach Road Port Dinorwic serves hot and cold bar food.

The Vaynol Arms (Inde Coope) in Pentir, serves bar meals and real ale. It has a beer terrace.

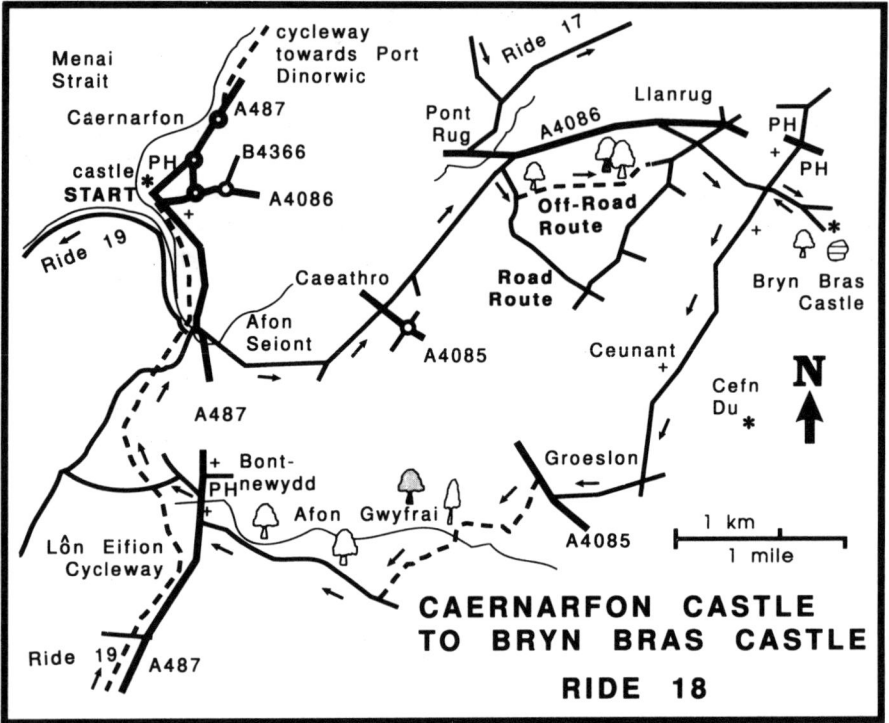

Menai Strait

Caernarfon

cycleway towards Port Dinorwic

A487

B4366

castle
START

PH

A4086

Ride 19

Ride 17

Pont Rug

A4086

Llanrug

PH

PH

Off-Road Route

Bryn Bras Castle

Caeathro

Afon Seiont

A4085

Road Route

Ceunant

Cefn Du

N

A487

Groeslon

Bont-newydd

PH

Afon Gwyfrai

A4085

1 km

1 mile

Lôn Eifion Cycleway

Ride 19

A487

CAERNARFON CASTLE
TO BRYN BRAS CASTLE

RIDE 18

RIDE 18

CAERNARFON CASTLE
TO BRYN BRAS CASTLE

ROUTE	Caernarfon—Caeathro—Pont Rug—Llanrug—Bryn Bras Castle—Ceunant—Groeslon—Afon Gwyrfai valley—Bontnewydd—via Lôn Eifion—Caernarfon
DISTANCE	13 miles/21 km
ASCENT	250 metres. From sea level to 205 metres at highest point. A good climb and an even better descent!
START	Caernarfon Castle car park or free one at start of cycleway, Grid Ref 480626.
TO START	Go down by the castle but turn left immediately before the paying car park into a road with small workshops. The free car park on the left on the disused railway has a height restriction.

It takes about 3 hours, which sounds slow for such a short ride but there are lots of off-road sections and there is one short sharp hill—well worth it for the lovely views, not to mention the long downhill sections on the last half of the route. It uses a RUPP to avoid the main road between Pont Rug and Llanrug, but I have briefly described the road alternative for those with lightweight bikes. We also use a good off-road track on a RUPP through the beautiful Afon Gwyrfai valley. This is well used by horse riders in summer so please be ready to give way to them. For the first ½ mile and the last mile we follow 2 branches of the excellent Lôn Eifion cycleway to and from Caernarfon.

If you want a longer ride there are links to Ride 19 in Caernarfon and to Ride 17 at Pont Rug. It is best done in late August when the heather is in bloom giving the rounded hills of Cefn Du and the distant Moel Rhiwen and Moel y Ci a rich purple colour.

THE RIDE

MAIN ROUTE 13 miles

If starting at **Caernarfon** castle paying car park, cycle away from it on the road past the workshops then along Lôn Eifion cycleway to the fork and turn left. Go over the little wooden bridge then under the road bridge. Turn left immediately through the stile. There is a small park here with toilets. There is no cycling but you can look at the duck pond. Turn left and ride up to the main road.

Turn left (it is safer using the pavement), cross the river, then take the first road on the left called Pen y Bryn and cycle up the wooded hill. It is a mile to the T-junction where you turn left. Pass large houses and enter **Caeathro** village passing the post office. Turn right, **with care**, onto the A4088 and immediately first left opposite the Bryngwrian pub. After ¼ mile turn left onto the main road. It is a mile to **Pont Rug**.

Just before here decide whether to do **Ride 17** as well—in which case continue to the main A4086, turn left onto it, cross the Seiont, and turn first right, **with care**, to join the other ride in ¼ mile as shown on the map.

MAIN ROUTE continued...
Turn first right on the bend, just before the main road onto a narrow lane. Decide on the Road or Off-Road Route.

ROAD ROUTE 2 miles
If you wish to stay **on road** (a mile further), to omit the next mile of off-road you would have to continue on this lane to a minor crossroads and turn left. Follow this lane for another mile to rejoin the track coming in on the left.

OFF-ROAD ROUTE 1 mile
This is safer, more fun, has possibilities of a picnic stop but is harder work! Turn first left onto a RUPP at Plas Tirion Lodge through wrought iron gates. The cart track is stony at first. Fork left onto a grassy track at Glantfor. It is gently uphill through a delightful wooded valley with a stream on the right. It is muddy in places and quite hard low gear work for ½ mile. Follow the track left by a caravan park where the surface improves. There are excellent views of the mountains from this pretty lane which passes Eglwys Sant Mihangel/St Michael's at the outskirts of **Llanrug**. At the lane at the end turn left (in a straight-on direction). The **Road Route** rejoins from the right.

MAIN ROUTE continued...
After 200 yards at the small cross roads turn right into Ffordd Minffordd. It is ½ mile to the cross roads (Bryngwyn). Go straight across following the signs for a visit to **Bryn Bras Castle** (see Other Information) or right, signed Waenfawr and Ceunant, to continue the ride. This point is 5½ miles from the start.

There is a bench soon before the start of the ascent. Then on the left is a terrace house with the biggest garden gnome I have ever seen! Go straight on for ½ mile then climb uphill—the steepest ascent is only for ¼ mile. Time to notice the farm animals: there is a good variety in this area including sheep, goats, donkeys, Welsh, Jersey and even Highland cattle. From the hill there are stupendous views across the strait to Anglesey. On a clear day you can see Newborough Warren. Pass the old Ceunant chapel dating from 1887. The highest point on the ride is reached by the aerial on the slopes of **Cefn Du** at approximately 205 metres.

Pass the track leading to Chamois Mountain Centre (Plas y Celyn and Beacon Climbing Wall) then turn right at the cross roads in **Groeslon** just after the start of the descent. There is an exhilarating glide down this straight road but be ready to stop at the main road at the bottom. Turn right, **with care**, onto the A4085 and in less than ¼ mile first left signed Snowdonia Riding Stables. Bear right at Weir Clodd Fawr by the stable entrance. Keep right by Caemybrynyr. Pass the fields of horses who like cyclists' apples! At the cross roads of tracks turn left steeply downhill into the bottom of the wooded valley. Cross the Afon Gwyrfai on the bridleway bridge and through the gate which has an obligingly high clasp for horse riders—handy for cyclists too. There is a short stony uphill track. Go through the farm gate, closing it of course. Bear left onto the asphalted road. It has a concrete surface for a bit then tarmac again and some of it is unfenced. Go through the final gate and turn right onto the minor road at a T-junction. Go over the tiny humpback bridge beside a stream. The bridge goes over a long-since disused railway.

Go downhill on this very pleasant lane flanked with old hedges of hazel. Pass the Libanus Chapel (1867). Turn right, **with care**, onto the main road into **Bontnewydd**. Cross the river and pass the Newborough Arms on the right. Pass Ysgol y Cynghor, a telephone, and the Siloam Chapel (1840). Turn left at the first junction into Dôl Beuno and pass a fish and chip shop. It is a pleasant winding lane with a stream beside the gardens on the left. At the first bridge turn right (dismount) and climb up the path to turn right onto the cycleway. It is one of the best sections of the Lôn Eifion track and is a delightful mile gently downhill to finish the back at Caernarfon.

Lôn Eifion

OTHER INFORMATION

CAERNARFON

Some of the medieval walls remain enclosing the castle and part of the town. **St Mary's Church** is 14th century and built into a corner of the walls. There are some 17th and 18th century houses and in Castle Square, opposite the statue of **Lloyd George**, are some Georgian buildings. There are also several old pubs. The **Tourist Information Centre** is on the ground floor of the council offices on Castle Street. The **Maritime Museum** is at Doc Victoria and covers maritime history. You can go on board Seiont II, a coal-fired steam dredger. Small charge for adults, children free. Open 11-4 Whit to September, tel 01286 675269. **Oriel Pendeitch** houses various exhibitions. It is in a terrace of cottages opposite the castle entrance. **Segontium Roman Fort** Museum is ten minutes from the centre. The Fort was occupied from AD78 for 400 years. It has maps and models and outside you can see the excavated remains of the fort. There are **Pleasure Boat Cruises** on board either Queen of the Sea or Snowdon Queen from the Quayside from May to Oct, tel 01286 672772. **Coed Helen** is a public park over the river with tennis courts, miniature golf, etc. **South Road Park** has wooded grounds and an ornamental lake with ducks.

Bryn Bras Castle

CAERNARFON CASTLE

This is undoubtedly Edward's finest castle in a striking setting the Seiont estuary with the Menai Strait. It was started in 1283 and completed in 1327. Previously on the site was a Norman motte and bailey castle dating from the 11th century. It has had a long and interesting history and is well worth a visit to find out more. It is run by CADW, tel 01286 77617.

BRYN BRAS CASTLE

This is a Grade 2 listed building. It was built in 1830 in Romanesque style, probably designed by Thomas Hopper who was building Penrhyn Castle at the time. There are gardens and also a pleasant woodland and short hill walk. It has a tearoom. It is open from Whit to September on Tuesdays to Fridays and Bank holiday Monday and Sunday from 1-5. From mid-July to end of August open from 11. Admission charge. It is privately owned and occupied. There is a holiday flat for those who would like residence in a castle!

THE PUBS

Lots of pubs and cafes in Caernarfon.

The Bryngwrian (Burtonwood) in Caeathro has a family room and beer garden. Newborough Arms (Tetley) in Bontnewydd serves bar meals and has picnic tables but involves crossing over a main road.

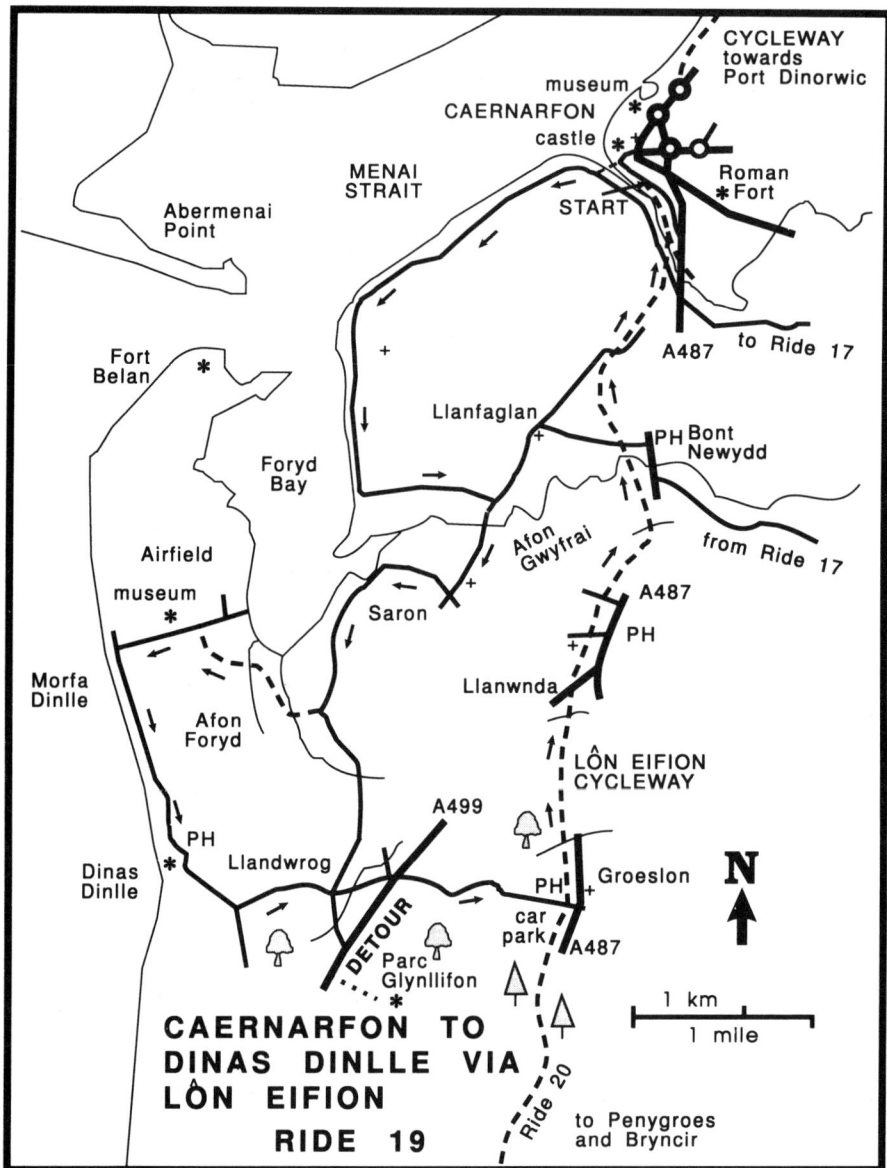

CYCLEWAY
towards
Port Dinorwic

museum
CAERNARFON
castle

*
*+

Roman
* Fort

MENAI
STRAIT

START

Abermenai
Point

A487   to Ride 17

Fort
Belan   *

+

Llanfaglan

PH Bont
Newydd

Foryd
Bay

+

Afon
Gwyfrai

from Ride 17

Airfield

museum
*

Saron

+

A487

+   PH

Morfa
Dinlle

Afon
Foryd

Llanwnda

LÔN EIFION
CYCLEWAY

A499

PH

Llandwrog

PH

Groeslon

+

N

Dinas
Dinlle
*

car
park   A487

DETOUR

Parc
Glynllifon
*

1 km

1 mile

CAERNARFON TO
DINAS DINLLE VIA
LÔN EIFION
RIDE 19

Ride 20

to Penygroes
and Bryncir

142

RIDE 19

CAERNARFON TO DINAS DINLLE VIA LÔN EIFION

ROUTE	Caernarfon—Llanfaglan—Saron—Morfa Dinlle—Dinas Dinlle—Llandwrog—(Glynllifon)—Groeslon—Lôn Eifion—Llanwnda—Bontnewydd—Caernarfon
DISTANCE	15 miles/24 km
ASCENT	80 metres. Flat.
START	Caernarfon Castle car park or free one at start of cycleway, Grid Ref 480626.
TO START	Go down by the castle but turn left immediately before the paying car park into a road with small workshops. The car park on the left on the disused railway has a height restriction.

This is an excellent ride for families and for off-road enthusiasts—a firm favourite. The outward route to Dinas Dinlle is on delightful lanes by the sea and the return from Groeslon to Caernarfon is via the Lôn Eifion cycleway. Anyone with young children wishing to avoid roads could simply go out and back on the cycleway.

THE RIDE

MAIN ROUTE 15 miles

From the free car park turn right along the road past the old foundry and workshops. Pass Castle Hill gift shop and the castle. Ride through the paying car park and along the quay. It is a busy and interesting harbour with many yachts to see and often 'seven swans a-swimming'.

Just before the town wall and the sea cross the river by the swing bridge (pedestrians and cycles only). Turn right and follow the coast road. There are fantastic views over the strait to Abermenai Point and Anglesey. There is a park on the left followed by a golf course. After 2 miles there is a chapel (Saint Baglan) in an isolated position in a field.

Another stunning ¾ mile along Foryd Bay, with many saltmarsh birds, brings you to a sharp bend away from the coast and a gentle uphill mile to a T-junction. There is a right turn and then a welcome glide down to cross the crystal-clear River Gwyrfai via Pont Faen.

St Baglan's church

After ½ mile enter the little village of Saron and pass its church dating from 1901. Pass a telephone box and turn first right at a cross roads. It is downhill to the coast again. The lane is very quiet and runs alongside an undisturbed reedbed and saltmarsh at the head of Foryd Bay. There are only a few houses, one of which has a punt, whose shallow draught is ideal for the shallow meandering watercourse. Again there are many birds .

After bending away from the sea there is a T-junction at which you turn right. In ½ mile there is a bend with a footpath crossing, just after this are the iron gates of Blythe Farm. Turn right through them onto the unsurfaced track and pass the **Snowdon Craft Workshops**. Continue past some derelict buildings to the gate and go through the gap on its left. Cross the Afon Carrog and follow the surfaced road for ¾ mile beside the marshy pools of the Afon Foryd. At the T-junction turn left. (To the right here is a caravan park at Morfa Lodge and also the way to Fort Belan, but this is unfortunately closed to the public at present.)

Pass the **Caernarfon Airport and Museum**. It is only ½ mile now to the sea at **Morfa Dinlle**. Bend sharp left by the toilets and there is a mile along the seafront with numerous access points to the steeply shelving beach for picnics etc. There are several cafes here. The road bends away from the coast in front of the towering mound of Dinas Dinlle. It is ½ mile gently uphill. Turn first left, signed Caernarfon and Pwllheli. It is ½ mile up a short hill to the attractive village of **Llandwrog**. Pass the post office, the coastguard's house, the Harp Inn/Westy Ty'n Llan (there is a poem on the wall in Welsh and English) and the church of St Twrog which has a tall steeple. Decide on the detour to Glynllifon or not.

MAIN ROUTE

Turn left immediately past the church, signed Ffordd Gûl/Single Track Road. This is a very quiet lane lined with old trees. Where it dips down to cross the stream it is worth gathering speed because of course it is uphill after the hollow! At the T-junction by the post box turn right and in a few yards at the main road go straight across the A499, **with great care**, into Lôn Cefn Glyn.

OR DETOUR TO GLYNLLIFON

Continue for ½ mile straight along the road from Llandwrog to the A499. Turn right, **with great care**, and immediately left into the entrance of Glynllifon Country Park. After visiting turn right, **with great care**, back onto the main road and follow it for ½ mile to turn first right, **with care**, into Lôn Cefn Glyn.

MAIN ROUTE continued...

This lane climbs up for about a mile following the stone boundary wall of the Glynllifon estate. If you go as slowly as I do up the hills you will probably have a chance to admire the tops of the trees! They are quite varied but mainly coniferous. There were even golden pheasants to spot in the fields on the left. From the top of this hill it is good news—it's downhill all the way back into Caernarfon.

In the village of Groeslon the cycleway is reached just before the main road (the A487). The pub on the corner, according to its sign, at one time had a landlord with a bald head and so the pub was alternatively known as Pen Nionyn/The Bald Head. There is an old Boundary Post beside the pub for the disused railway and is labelled L & NW Ry Co. Coming up the lane turn left through the gate onto the cycleway. It is wide enough here for two to cycle abreast and it has a good tarmac surface to the next junction. Here the pub is Y Goat just down the road to the left. There are also some very old petrol pumps. The cycleway continues on a narrow gravelled track. Unfortunately it then crosses the rather busy A499. Go through the gate back onto the old railway. It is a gravelled surface and is single file. The next minor road crossing is Glanrhyd in **Llanwnda** village. If you wish to visit the old church turn left.

Continue on the cycleway and the next road crosses on a bridge. Immediately after this on the left there is a Norman chapel with a huge urn outside. Several gated cart-tracks cross in the next section but there are special openings for cyclists. On the outskirts of **Bontnewydd** we cross the Afon Gwyrfai (seen earlier on the outward route). There is a beautiful wooded valley next with ash, hazel and sycamore with harts tongue fern beneath and some wild flowers such as meadowsweet, hardheads, groundsel and toadflax. There are also more open sections with glimpses of the hills of the Lleyn Peninsula.

Returning to Caernarfon along Lôn Eifion

Cross a narrow lane, by the house called Hendy, and there is another lovely wooded stretch. The route then crosses an impressive bridge over the River Seiont far below. A branch of another disused railway comes in on the right. It is possible to do a pleasant, but short, there-and-back detour along this (crossing the river by the A487 road bridge) as far as a park to see the ducks, but cycling is forbidden.

The cycleway continues back to Caernarfon through a grove of purple buddleias whose sweet scent almost masks the unpleasant odours from the sewage works and gasworks below. The route returns to the car park with impressive views of the castle ahead.

OTHER INFORMATION

For Caernarfon see Ride 18

CAERNARFON AIRPORT AND MUSEUM

Short pleasure flights in a light aircraft can be taken by the brave! There is a small museum with a flight simulator and the story of the RAF Mountain Rescue, tel 01286 830800.

PARC GLYNLLIFON

The grounds of the Agricultural College are open to the public. There are beautiful paths through woodland, field and streamside as well as some more formally planted areas. You can visit Lord Newborough's 18th century fort, look round the Victorian workshops and see a collection of old tools and a steam engine restored by Fred Dibnah. There is a programme of events including performances staged in the open air theatre in summer. At the craft workshops you can see the work of local potters, artists and designers. It has a small gift shop and a tearoom selling good home made food open from 11. Footpaths are open all year. Exhibitions are open at Easter and from Whit to September from 10-5. The grounds are free but there is a small charge for the exhibitions, tel 01286 830222.

LLANFAGLAN

Like many other medieval churches in the area there is no sign of the community St Baglan once must have served. It is in a splendid isolated position a short stroll across the field from the shore. The site may have been an ancient place of worship as there are Roman stones in its walls and the door lintel is actually a Roman tombstone. It was conveyed to the Friends of Friendless Churches in 1991. They maintain it with voluntary donations.

FORT BELAN

This was built by the first Lord Newborough in the late 18th century to defend the entrance to the Menai Strait from possible invasion by the French. It has impressive cannons. The fort was designed to match the one called Fort Williamsburg in the grounds of Glynllifon which is open. I visited Fort Belan many years ago when it was open to the public but it is closed at present.

MORFA DINLLE AND DINAS DINLLE

There is a straight mainly shingle beach and at the far end is the fascinating mound of Dinas Dinlle. It was originally an early British defended hill and then the site of a Roman fortress with double ramparts. The Romans also built a causeway joining it to their Segontium fortress at Caernarfon and thus it was the seaward end of Watling Street. LLANDWROG

The village was built by Lord Newborough in Gothic style in the early 19th century. There are attractive almshouses and the church has a prominent spire. We go past the Snowdon Craft Workshops at Blythe Farm which are worth a visit when

open to see the models being made of unusual but locally appropriate slate and resin.

INIGO JONES TUDOR SLATEWORKS
The slate showroom is open to the public and in summer there is an audio self-guided tour of the works also a small cafe. See Ride 20.

LLANWNDA
This village has a Romanesque church and a Victorian chapel in gothic style with an octagonal spire, Capel Glanrhyd, dating from 1899.

THE RIVALS
The mountains of the Lleyn or Llyn are properly called Yr Eifl in Welsh meaning 'The Fork'. The English 'Rivals' is a corruption.

THE PUBS
The Anglesey Hotel (Marstons) is in Caernarfon
The Harp Inn/Westy Ty'n Llan is in Llandwrog
The Llanfair Arms (Marstons) and Pen Nionyn/The Bald Head are in Groeslon
Y Goat (Bass) between Groeslon and Llanwnda.

GROESLON TO BRYNCIR VIA LÔN EIFION

ROUTE	Groeslon—Bryncir via cycleway and back, or return via Bwlch derwin—Aberdesach—Pont y Cim—Penygroes—Groeslon
DISTANCE	19 miles/30 km, including Road Return Route of 11½ miles. Short Cut, 17½ miles. Or, Lôn Eifion there-and-back 15 miles/24 km.
ASCENT	60 metres, ie almost nil on Lôn Eifion. Road Return Route is hilly, 150 metres.
START	Groeslon public car park by Llanfair Arms on A487, Grid Ref 473559.
TO START	From Caernarfon take the A487 south towards Porthmadog for 3 miles to Llanwnda. Fork left, still on A487, 1½ miles to Groeslon. Car park on right.

For young children I would recommend returning on the cycleway but for others wanting an almost circular round trip the return via the lanes on the Road Route is interesting if rather hilly. I prefer visiting the beach at Aberdesach on the return route as it is only 1½ miles further than the Short Cut. It uses very quiet lanes but does have just under ½ mile on a main road. The Short Cut has no main road. Beware of glass on the cycleway especially around Penygroes. There is also a lane parallel to the cycleway between Nazareth and Pant Glas (see Map) for those who don't like the rough surface and the gates on this part of the cycleway at present. You would have to cross the A487 to reach it. It climbs a little and contours round the foot of Mynydd Graig Goch. For a longer route you could link with Ride 19 at Groeslon.

THE RIDE
OUTWARD ROUTE ON LÔN EIFION 7½ miles
From the car park in Groeslon turn left onto the cycleway. It is ½ mile to the Slate Works. There is a rear entrance via a small gate. Next is a wooded area with alders and oaks. A cart track crosses then the cycleway follows the impressive stone wall of Glynllifon with conifer plantations inside. There is

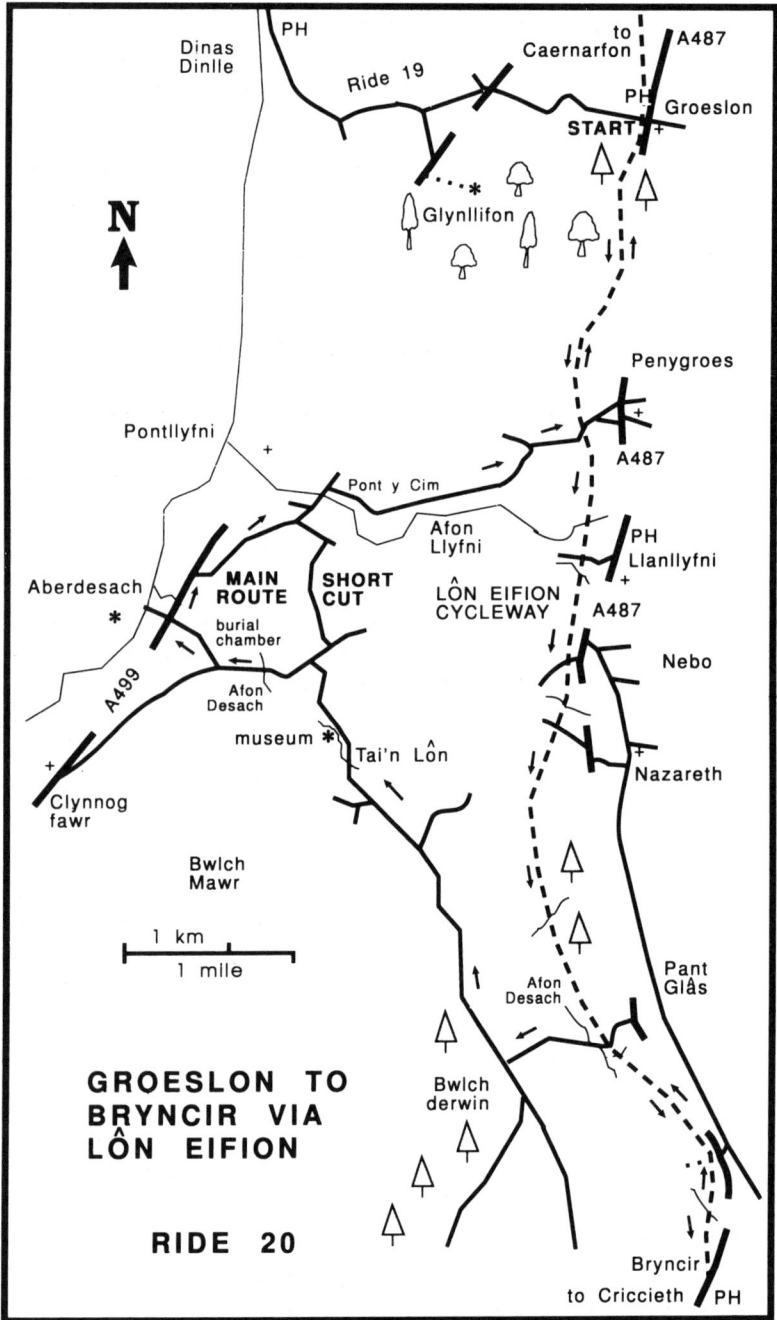

Dinas Dinlle

PH

Ride 19

to Caernarfon

A487

PH   Groeslon

START

N

Glynllifon

Penygroes

A487

Pontllyfni

Pont y Cim

Afon Llyfni

PH Llanllyfni

Aberdesach

MAIN ROUTE

SHORT CUT

LÔN EIFION CYCLEWAY

A487

burial chamber

Nebo

A499

Afon Desach

museum

Tai'n Lôn

Nazareth

Clynnog fawr

Bwlch Mawr

1 km

1 mile

Afon Desach

Pant Glâs

GROESLON TO BRYNCIR VIA LÔN EIFION

Bwlch derwin

RIDE 20

Bryncir

to Criccieth   PH

a damp hollow on the left with a stream and bog vegetation such as meadowsweet. After the telegraph wires, the view suddenly opens towards the mountains with Bwlch Mawr ahead and the sea on the right. There is a slight rise to Penygroes.

Penygroes has an old railway station with access to the road on either side. It is then ½ mile to a high bridge over the valley of the Llyfni. There are a couple more road bridges, one over and one under, and then you could find a good picnic spot with views over the strait to Newborough sands and Llanddwyn Island.

Next are conifer plantations producing mainly spruce, then a large quarry and a road crossing for the quarry. The tarmac now ends and is replaced by shingly gravel. There is a large TV mast on the left. After an old signal box the track is single file. There is one stream immediately and then another three: of these, the first and third have easy access for picnics. The track is double width for a short distance on the embankment. Next is a cattle crossing, then two easy gates, followed by a proper road crossing between Pant Glâs to the left and Bwlch derwin to the right.

The track goes under pylons then through a well designed gate. The way is now narrow and grassy. There are a couple of gates, please be sure to shut them as sheep sometimes find their way through the fence and onto the cyclepath. The path runs beside the road for a while. There is an old bridge over a rushing stream then a concrete farm track. The next bridge is over a stream which looks as if it would make a good picnic place, but don't try it as it is surrounded by a tangle of barbed wire. Wait for the next bridge which is ideal and accessible.

Then at the agricultural implement workshop at **Bryncir** the cycletrack ends. If you go onto the main road and cross it, **with extreme care**, you will find a garage selling ice creams and soft drinks as does the garden centre a few yards further (this is on the cycletrack side of the road so you could just walk along the pavement to it). The pub here is the Bryncir Arms.

RETURN VIA LÔN EIFION 7½ miles
Return initially via the cycleway, passing the gates, the 3 streams and pylons, to the old signal box, which would make a useful shelter if caught out in bad weather. Here decide whether to return on the cycleway or by roads. Simply retrace the outward route if you wish to avoid roads.

ROAD RETURN ROUTE 11½ miles
Turn left onto the road. It is ¼ mile uphill to a footpath sign at the top of the hill then downhill to a sharp right bend, signed Tai'n Lôn, Capel Uchaf and Clynnog Fawr. (The sign for the museum is a wagon on a brown

background.) There is an old National school Ysgol y Cynghor (1908). The lane goes more gently downhill and passes a trekking centre (Ynys Yr Arch Clynnogfawr). Pass a willowy hollow. This has dangerous quick sands and reclaimed gravel pits. Go straight on past a lane off to the right by a tip entrance, which used to be an old quarry. Go steeply down and turn first right, **with care**, on a very steep downhill section.

Carry on down to **Tai'n Lôn** and an old smithy Yr Hen Efail (which used to have old farm wagons, pump, mill stone and bits of ancient agricultural implements—but these have recently gone to the museum). The next track to the left goes to the **Museum of Welsh Life**, it crosses a shallow ford. The museum is worth a short visit. Return to the lane and turn left. Continue to the T-junction (sign pointing back to Tai'n Lôn, Bwlch derwin, Pont-Glâs and left to Clynnog Fawr). Decide here whether to do the Short Cut or to continue on the Main Route through Aberdesach.

SHORT CUT... 1½ miles shorter
Turn right at this T-junction and go uphill for only ¼ mile. Turn first left. Follow this narrow lane downhill for a mile and rejoin the Main Route at * just before Pont y Cim.

MAIN ROUTE VIA ABERDESACH...
Turn left at this T-junction and cycle down to the stream and then steeply up the other side. After ½ mile turn first right (unsigned) along a very narrow lane lined with trees. There are wild flowers in spring such as celandine, stitchwort and a few primroses and violets. There is also a collapsed burial chamber in the field on the right. Pass the large greenhouses of Aberdesach nurseries. Almost immediately the lane drops down to the main road so be ready to stop! Cross, **with care**, into another narrow lane to the tiny seaside village of **Aberdesach**.

Near Aberdesach

There is a shop selling ice creams, teas and coffees. It is worth going down to see the wide sweep of the bay with views across to Anglesey and Holy Island to the right and the mountains of the Lleyn to the left. It is a pebbly beach and makes a good spot for a picnic or just a short breather. There is a car park, picnic tables and public toilets and so would make an alternative start.

Return to the main road, the A499, and turn left onto it for ½ mile. Turn first right, **with care**. This is a lovely lane and has splendid views of Snowdon. After Brynaerau Chapel (1879) turn left at the T-junction **(* the Short Cut rejoins here)** and right on the next bend and go across the ancient **Pont y Cim** and turn immediately right. It is 1¼ miles along a lovely lane to a T-junction. Turn right towards **Penygroes** to return to the cycleway for the last lap back to Groeslon. Cross the bridge over the cycleway (the pub Yr Afr is in sight ahead), turn first right, signed cycleway, and turn right onto it.

Pont y Cim

(If you visit **Penygroes** first before returning to the cycleway you will see the Victoria pub, a Chinese restaurant and public toilets. Along Snowdon Street/Stryd yr Wyddfa there is also a telephone, a cross, a fish and chip shop, and Yr Afr pub. Return along Station Road back to the cycleway at the old station. Turn right onto the cycleway.)

It is a pleasant 2 miles return, passing the slateworks and its cafe again, and so back to the beginning of the route at **Groeslon**.

OTHER INFORMATION

INIGO JONES SLATE WORKS

This was started in 1861 originally to make school writing slates. Today there is a variety of products all made of slate and you can watch the craftsmen making steps, worktops, hearths, flooring and craft items. There are self-guided tours and exhibitions of letter-cutting and calligraphy and a children's quiz. Open from Easter to September, weekdays 9-5, weekends 10-5. October to Easter, Mon-Thu 9-4.30, Fri 9-3.30, tel 01286 830242.

MUSEUM OF OLD WELSH LIFE/FELIN FAESOG

This is housed in a 17th century watermill in the tiny village of Tai'n Lôn. Visiting by bike is fun if you enjoy a quick splash while crossing the ford through the stream, the Afon Desach. It has displays depicting everyday Welsh life of the era of the mill. It also has a small tearoom. It has been open 10-5 daily except Saturday, but as it has irregular opening it might be best to phone first, tel 01286 86311.

PONT Y CIM

This ancient bridge dates from 1612 and is only about 7 feet wide—plenty of room for cyclists but not appropriate for modern traffic. It was the lowest bridging point over the Afon Llyfni and carried the traffic down the Lleyn until the main road was built through Pontllyfni.

LLEYN PENINSULA

This part of the Lleyn has a coastline and terrain similar for cyclists to that of Anglesey. The coastal strip is fairly flat and there are dramatic seaward and mountain views everywhere. The only busy resorts are to the south of our routes towards the tip of the peninsula.

THE PUBS

Llanfair Arms in Groeslon.
Bryncir Arms (Whitbread) in Bryncir serves bar meals and has picnic tables.
The Victoria and Yr Afr (the Goat) (Greenalls) are both in Penygroes.

SUGGESTIONS FOR OTHER RIDES

ROAD ROUTES

Llandudno Junction—Hendre Wen—Pen y Bont—detour to Penrhyn Bay and Rhos—Penrhyn side—detour to Craig y don and Llandudno—B5115—Llanrhos—Tyn y Coed—RUPP to Pydew—Pabo—Esgryn—Llandudno Junction. Quiet lanes, fairly flat.

Conwy—Groesffordd—Henryd—Glyn Isa—Roewen—Caerhun (Canovium Roman Fort)—B5106—Tyn y groes—B5279—(Tal y cafn)—River Conwy—Tremorfa—hospital—Fachleidiog—Gyffin—Conwy. Quiet lanes, quite hilly.

Colwyn Bay hinterland. Quiet lanes, fairly flat.

Ruthin to Denbigh in the Denbigh Valley Pleasant quiet lanes, fairly flat.

Blaenau Ffestiniog to Porthmadog Take the narrow gauge railway uphill and cycle/freewheel back downhill. Mostly main roads, often rains! Only room for 2 or 3 bikes on the train, small charge.

OFF-ROAD ROUTES

Beddgelert Forest and the forest at Betws y Coed

There are some excellent forest tracks on which you can cycle safely away from traffic. For mountain bike enthusiasts this is ideal and some tracks are quite hilly. For bike hire see the chapter on Design of Routes. It is best to start in the Beddgelert Forest between Beddgelert and Rhyd-Ddu on the A4085, signed Forest Walks, at Pont Cae'r-Gors. Tracks in the Hafod Ruffydd, Cwm Cloch and Meillionen area are good. The bridleway which goes over Cwm Trwsgl to Cwm Pennant is totally unsuitable for cycling.

Snowdon

Some of the paths are bridleways. There is an agreed voluntary ban by all the cycling organisations on cycling on Snowdon from 1st June to 30th September. The first year of the ban, 1993, was very successful—there was only a twelfth of the number of cyclists recorded at the summit compared with before. Hopefully this will also cut down on the accident rate. In that year three mountain-bikers had to be airlifted off the mountain following accidents, and one died. In my opinion it is unwise to cycle on Snowdon and similar mountains, as the conditions can be very treacherous. It is also anti-social, as the number of walkers on popular peaks like Snowdon is now so high that conflict is unavoidable. It is bad environmentally, as on steep paths without hard surfaces cycling can lead to erosion. There are much better trails through the forests on more suitable and quieter tracks.

Llyn Ogwen to Capel Curig RUPP along Afon Llugwy 4 miles, rough track.

Llyn Cowlyd 4 miles, bridleway. Very hilly: about 500 metres ascent, very rough path, very boggy, mountain environment. Could cause erosion.

Llanfairfechan to Penmaenmawr (5 miles) or Sychnant Pass (6 miles) RUPP and bridleway. Very hilly, rough, wet, mountain environment.

In Beddgelert Forest

REFERENCES

Ordnance Survey Sheets 114 Anglesey, 115 Snowdon and Surrounding Area and 116 Denbigh and Colwyn Bay (Landranger Series).

Lôn Eifion Cycleway - council leaflet

SUSTRANS leaflets

The Rivers of Anglesey, Gwilym T Jones, 1989, UCNW Research Centre.

The New Welsh Dictionary, H Meurig Evans and W O Thomas, Christopher Davies, 1953.

USEFUL ADDRESSES

Anglesey Coastal Heritage, Llys Llewelyn, Tyddyn Hwrdd, Aberffraw, tel 01407 840845

North Wales Wildlife Trust, 376 High Street, Bangor, tel 01248 351545

Ordnance Survey, Romsey Road, Southampton, SO9 4DH, tel 01703 792000

Cycle Shops in the area:
West End Cycles, 33-5 High Street, Bangor

Mike's Bikes, 33 Holyhead Road, Upper Bangor

Don's Bikes, 47 Pool Street, Caernarfon

DRP Owen, Dorset Sports Stores, Kingsland, Holyhead

Ray Goy, Newborough, manufacturer of cycling hardware accessories, tel 01248 440365

SUSTRANS:
35, King Street, Bristol, BS1 4DZ (cyclepath Charity) send SAE & donation for leaflets/membership.

Cycling Project for the North West:
Environmental Institute, Bolton Road, Swinton, Manchester M27 2UX, tel 0161 7941926

Cyclists' Touring Club:
Cotterell House, 69, Meadrow, Godalming, Surrey.

Cycle Campaign Network:
Tress House, Stamford Street, London, tel 0171-928 7220

Friends of the Earth:
26-28, Underwood Street, London, tel 0171-490 1555

OTHER READING

Family Cycling in North Cheshire and Nearby Areas, Lyn Goodkin, Alfresco Books, 7 Pineways, Appleton, Warrington, 1992

Family Cycling in West Cheshire and Wirral, Lyn Goodkin, Hobbyhorse Books, The Old Post Office, Chester Road, Daresbury, Warrington, WA4 4AJ, 1994

CTC Book of Cycling, John Whatmore, David & Charles, 1983

Richard's Bicycle Book, Richard Ballantine, Pan, 1975

New Natural History of Anglesey, ed W Eifion Jones, Anglesey Antiquarian Society, 1991

Mona Enchanted Island, Geoffrey Eley, Priory Press, 1968

The Golden Wreck—the Tragedy of the Royal Charter, Alex McKee, Hodder and Stoughton

Place Names (in Welsh), Bedwyr Lewis Jones

Welsh Place-names and their Meanings, Dewi Davies

Lifelines 10, Thomas Telford, Rhoda M. Pearce, Shire 1972 and 1978